COLOR

IN THE AMERICAN HOME

COLOR

IN THE AMERICAN HOME

Margaret Sabo Wills

CREATIVE HOMEOWNER®, Upper Saddle River, New Jersey

Editorial Director: Timothy O. Bakke
Art Director: Annie Jeon

Editor: Lynn Elliott
Decorating Books Editor: Kathie Robitz
Copyeditor: Diane Hodges
Indexer: Sandi Schroeder

Design and Layout: Jan H. Greco
Illustrator: Vincent Alessi

Front Cover Design: Annie Jeon
Front Cover Photography: Melabee M Miller
Slipcovers: Farhi and del Rio
Fabric: Courtesy of Waverly

Back Cover Design: Jan H. Greco
Back Cover Photography (clockwise): Rob Melnychuk,
Alan Shortall, Rob Melnychuk

Manufactured in the United States of America

Current Printing (last digit)
10 9 8 7 6 5 4 3

Color in the American Home, First Edition
Library of Congress Catalog Card Number: 97-075268
ISBN: 1-58011-010-X

CREATIVE HOMEOWNER®
A Division of Federal Marketing Corp.
24 Park Way
Upper Saddle River, NJ 07458
Web site: **www.creativehomeowner.com**

Dedication

Sentiment comes first—

This book is dedicated to my colorful family: my mother and father, who gave me the world; my siblings Bonnie, John, Shawn, Jim, Teresa, and Jennifer; my cherished children Rosalind and Benedict, who amaze me every day; Anita and Chill, Cynthia and Carroll, who have welcomed me in; and most of all, my beloved husband Stewart, the joy of my heart.

Acknowledgments

Business comes next—

Thank you to all the people who so freely shared aesthetic insights and hard information on this fascinating topic. These include Margaret Walch, director of the Color Association of the United States, and co-author, with Augustine Hope, of the delightful and fact-filled *Color Compendium* and *In Living Color*; design historian Gail Caskey Winkler; Catherine Stein, president of the Color Council; the helpful folks at the Color Marketing Group, including Melanie Wood; Munsell Color; Pantone Inc.; and the designers who shared a few of their observations and methods with me—Sue Calvin, Rebecca Ewing, Christopher Drake and Lee Bierly, Lori Erenberg, Pia Ledy, Robert Orr, Lyn Peterson, and Gretchen Rhodes, and all the others whose work invigorates these pages. A special nod, too, to my hard-working editors, Lynn Elliott and Kathie Robitz. And thank you to all the readers out there working at various aspects of making a home.

—*Margaret Sabo Wills*

CONTENTS

I N T R O D

Whether you envision your house in austere Shaker forms, opulent Deco curves, country collectibles, or formal symmetries, you're no doubt daydreaming in color. Color has always been the decorator's most personal, versatile, and evocative tool. It establishes a room's character—elegant or offbeat, restful or energetic. And while some decorating dreams fall under the budget's ax, imaginative and satisfying colors generally cost no more than pedestrian choices. Used strategically, color can visually reshape a space to feel less constrained, more cozy, or better proportioned. Particular hues also embody a design style: You can't furnish an authentic New England saltbox house in bouncy 1950s pastels or a retro-fifties Miami kitchen in grayed Nantucket green.

The oldest design traditions reflect eras when a homeowner was limited to locally avail-able pigments and dyes. When trade developed, it often pursued exotic fabrics, jewelry, and splendid furnishings—a quest for color. America began as a narrow string of colonies open to a wide ocean of influences. We've never been tied to one style, and our many-layered history, diverse ethnic traditions, and lively regional differences still present a rich palette of choices. Combine that history with technology developed in recent decades, and you realize that we're awash in color to an unprecedented degree—we casually skim and toss away vivid magazines, we snap photos in colors a master painter would admire, or we watch TV, films, and computer screens in glowing hues. Homeowners in other times

and places would envy the ease with which we spin rainbowlike racks of paint chips and flip through endless wallpaper books. All of design history is there for us to raid.

Yet that very richness can be daunting enough to make many homeowners retreat to safe, neutral territory. How comforting to know that this timidity is not new—a century ago, Victorian writer Oliver Coleman noted:

> *"Like a man who realizes he has not an acute and accurate ear for music, and hence in singing murmurs softly to himself, so most of us in dealing with the various combinations of reds and blues and yellows murmur in tints for fear that a sudden pause may find us shouting off the key and in another tune. This is, no doubt, why buff is almost always used for yellow, why green is sage, and crimson is but a mawkish pink."*

This is not to say that buff, sage, and pink can't be lovely, livable choices. A better moral to draw: Colors, whether subtle or dazzling, should be selected with an appreciation of

the possibilities—a joyful choosing, not a retreat from a real decision. Today's brimming smorgasbord of colors makes it all the more necessary for homeowners to decorate with a clear plan and a personal approach.

To that end, this book will show you how to use color as confidently as an interior designer. We'll start with a survey of palettes past—especially helpful to someone seeking a period flavor. Then we'll look abstractly at color and light to underpin some practical approaches for arriving at your color scheme. Three separate chapters celebrate warm, cool, and neutral choices, though colors don't always corral quite so neatly. A chapter on painted finishes suggests ways to inject color into a room. Finally, we'll consider the market forces that determine what your shopping trips yield. And along the way, "Design Secrets" will provide you with useful insider advice from professionals. Ultimately, this book aims to be your hands-on guide toward understanding and using *the power of the palette.*

a heritage to build upon

america's design history can provide color inspirations whether you're selecting hues for a regional, ethnic, or period flavor, or devising your own personal mix. In a house of character—a Georgian manor, a 1920s Florida "Deco dream," or a Craftsman bungalow—colors true to the era may look particularly fitting. If you're trying to give bland, boxy rooms a sense of the past, evocative hues can take you halfway there. "There's comfort in a palette that has the endorsement of history," notes color authority Margaret Walch. "It's all done for you—you're not trying to evolve what combinations might work together." Designers of museum period rooms invest hours microanalyzing old paints to determine just what those authentic hues might be.

Previous page: *A brick red exterior extends the welcome of a Colonial house.*

Below: *Buttery yellow walls frame delicate furniture, the type that was typically imported from Europe.*

Color palette: *The paint dabs in this chapter show each historic period's colors. Deep blue, verdigris, cane yellow, and earth red of the Colonial period.*

A homeowner, happily unfettered by the need for strict museum-quality accuracy, might choose colors and patterns that merely create a nostalgic mood or suggest an era's flavor instead of slavishly copying it.

colonial roots

The first waves of European settlers to America's shores in the early 1600s—whether the Spanish in Florida, the Dutch in New York, the French at the Canadian border, or the English dominating in New England and Virginia—focused on survival rather than décor. Their homes reflected the natural hues of the wood, stone, clay, and animal skins abundantly available, brightened by whatever furnishings might have been squeezed onto crowded ships.

By the 1700s, prosperous colonists aspired to finer houses with interiors brightened by plaster and whitewash, which was sometimes tinted with minerals. Fashionable homes were painted with imported powdered pigments mixed on-site with linseed oil or were finished in costly European wallpapers and fabrics. Upholstered easy chairs, a recent innovation, were covered in pastel damasks, brightly colored solid wool, or flame-stitch or scenic needle-

craft. Bright "turkeywork" embroidery imitated rare and much-prized Oriental rugs. While cavalierly lumping together the cultures of Japan, China, and India, colonists craved exotic Eastern fabrics, handpainted wallpapers, ceramics, and lacquered furniture, which brightened many sturdy New England settings.

European powers had envisioned the Colonies supplying cheap raw materials and buying back imported manufactured goods. But with the steady arrival of skilled artisans, America was soon making its own furniture. The Connecticut–Long Island coast was known for delicately painted chests and chairs; Boston for its "Japanned" pieces in lustrous red, black, and brown; and Philadelphia for its command of the latest fashions. By

Left: *Away from stylish cities, early Americans relied on their own ingenuity with natural dyes and earth pigments. Mellow colors, such as this plank door's russet red, can still summon up an easygoing country flavor.*

1730, Philadelphia merchant Plunket Fleeson was proudly advertising domestically produced wallpapers.

The early Colonial palette, influenced by British fashions, tended to be rich and muted with deep blues, gray-greens, and earthy reds and neutrals. But by the mid-eighteenth century, with English architects discovering Italy's sun-drenched colors and the highly publicized excavation of ancient and vividly painted Greek and Roman sites, neoclassicism was in the air. Styles turned toward sleeker, more delicately scaled furniture and lighter, brighter colors than previously seen.

Top left: *Native American rugs and blankets glow in cochineal red against a backdrop of whitewashed planks. The ornate turned-leg Spanish Revival chairs add a hint of formality to a vigorous Southwestern-style living room.*

Left: *An appealing array of Scandinavian blue tints from light to dark clearly reveals a rustic spirit in this children's bedroom. The use of natural wood tones and a folk tapestry warms up the predominantly blue scheme.*

Left: *Traditional needn't always be predictable— a Pennsylvania home-owner took inspiration from an Irish country manor in choosing the entry hall's lush rosy hue.*

Color palette: *A Wedgewood blue, Adam green, Turner's yellow, and buff of the Federal era.*

"A lot of late eighteenth- and early nineteenth-century colors were exceedingly intense," notes design historian Gail Caskey Winkler, "even though many people envision a wonderful era when everything was cream and dove gray." Misconceptions about Federal-era colors stem partly from the unstable, or "fugitive," nature of early paints. Modern laboratory analysis indicates that the palette's earthier side—the dun yellows, tans, and deeper Spanish brown and barn reds—came down to us in fairly true form. But some carefully uncovered paint layers are deceptive: A dark green might once have been bright Prussian blue, and a muddy brown originally a turquoise verdigris.

Above: *Some San Francisco homes of the Victorian era, dubbed "painted ladies," are now painted in multicolor schemes that may stray beyond historical precedent. Yet the treatment plays up the architecture and adds a high-spirited fillip to the modern urban scene.*

So instead of grayed-down "Colonial" tones, our founding fathers might have finished their best rooms in brilliant sky blue, salmon, strong yellow, or apple green, colors that would still make a stunning impression by dim candlelight.

different visions

Since such pigments were expensive, more subdued paints remained the norm away from the urban centers. Families living closer to the land tinted homespun wools and linens with home-brewed dyes, sometimes made more lasting with "mordants" of soda, salt, alum, or lye. Settlers added to their dye "receipts" by noting the roots, bark, flowers, and berries with which various American Indian cultures tinted their intricate quill-work and sinew-stitched leathers in rich yellow, red, blue, and black. Colonial women might embroider the bright vegetable-dyed yarns on imported linen-cotton fustian to make bold crewelwork bed hangings and dense bed rugs. After the 1800s, embroidery styles turned finer, and colorful samplers stitched in imported silks brightened many walls.

Though British styles and colors dominated the fashions, in 1790 only about sixty percent of North America's European population was of English descent. Scattered French trading posts led from Canadian enclaves down the Ohio and Mississippi Valleys to the stronghold of New Orleans, where

Creole French styles fostered fresh floral colors and ornamental ironwork. New Orleans also came under the Spanish influence that stretched from the Florida peninsula through to the Southwest. There, Spanish joined Native American in homes of smooth, pale adobe and stucco, rich with tones of rugged wood, touches of blue, dark orange, and cochineal red—a vivid dyestuff made from tiny insects that feed on cactuses.

In the mid-eighteenth century, Scandinavian settlers along the Delaware built America's first log cabins; there and in the upper

Top right: *Rustic cottages of the early twentieth century were an eclectic mix of influences. Here, the earthy tones of the Craftsman movement and the cochineal reds of the Native Americans create a country-cottage mood.*

Right: *In its exotic Anglo-Japanese style, this hall shows the Victorian love of color and pattern as it joins Oriental rugs, an all-over floral wallpaper, rich woodwork, and stained glass.*

Color palette: *Sun-baked brown, golden yellow, flannel red, and turquoise of the Southwest.*

design secret:
Don't always match a color exactly. Accessories in a lighter or related shade add visual interest and keep the scheme from being repetitious.

Midwest during the following century, they recreated northern Europe's cool pastel interiors with furniture painted in swirling florals. Pennsylvania, with its founding principles of religious toleration, attracted assorted nationalities during the eighteenth century. Included among them were several waves of German settlers, who decorated their houses in stylized motifs of hearts, tulips, birds, and scrolls in deep reds and blues on embroidered linens and painted furniture. Farther south, coastal cities, such as Charleston, opened to a cosmopolitan mix of imported fashions, while farther inland, farmers of Scottish, Irish, and Welsh descent held onto simpler old-country traditions in wool and linens.

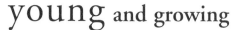

young and growing

Long after the Revolutionary War, America remained tied to European fashions—often French inspirations reflected through a British viewpoint. "We may have rebelled against Britain," quips Walch, "but we took all their furniture." The nineteenth century presented another kind of revolution, powered by new technology and new wealth. The expanding middle class could revel in factory-produced wallpapers and machine-made furniture.

The flood of mass-produced fabric, ironically, fostered the nineteenth-century peak for the colorfully individualistic and particularly American craft of quilting. Begun as thrifty use of precious fabric scraps, quilting soon became a medium

Above: *A Midwestern home handsomely reinterprets the Prairie Style, including its Oriental allusions. Fern-patterned taupe-on-beige wallpaper is enlivened by the claret-hued couch.*

Left: *Strong, unfussy outlines in natural woods, detailed with metalwork in copper and vivid stained glass, suggest an Arts and Crafts inspiration for a rugged family-style kitchen.*

for personal artistic expression. It was also a democratic craft: A New York matron might piece velvets; a pioneer woman, bright calicos. Certain quilts made by African-Americans during the slave era display bold, high-contrast figures and rectangular panels linked by design historians to West African appliquéd banners.

style-conscious
victorians

In the Victorian era, not only products but words were mass-produced, as magazines and books instructed an increasingly literate public on the finer points of taste. "It was an era that was eager to explain itself," notes historian Winkler. Early Victorian tastemakers advocated tuning color to the settings, with "sober" libraries, "cheerful" pastel bedrooms, and "gay" company parlors in pearl gray, vivid green, and misty "ashes of roses" pink.

Rooms were also richly patterned, with newly available wallcoverings, painted floors or floorcloths, and grained or marbled surfaces. Critics derided cold "cheerless" white walls as "painfully distressing to the eye"—a danger minimized by the era's rapidly developing color technology. In 1856, an eighteen-year-old English chemist's assistant, trying to synthesize quinine from coal tar, discovered a rich purple dye. It was christened "mauve" by the French, heralding a rainbow of synthetic aniline dyes. By the 1870s, premixed paints were readily available.

In the late nineteenth century, the palette turned richer and more saturated with dark green and red, ocher and russet, peacock blue and olive—complex colors not possible earlier. Design writers set forth "scientific" guidelines for combining large numbers of colors according to "Harmonies of Contrast" or

"Harmonies of Analogous Colors." Fashionable walls featured separate treatments for dado, upper wall, and frieze. Draperies also grew profuse and appeared not just as window dressings but as doorway portières and mantel lambrequins. Beds were left uncurtained, however, in the interest of "hygiene."

In 1876, almost one-quarter of the population attended Philadelphia's World Fair and Centennial celebration. This burst of national pride promoted a nostalgic Colonial revival, entailing lighter colors, reclaimed antiques, and reproduction wallpapers. But revivals of all kinds had been in the air—stylish Victorian rooms might be Gothic, Moorish, Greco-Egyptian, even Native American, or evoke the era of the Renaissance or Louis XIV through XVI, often with more atmosphere than accuracy.

fresh approaches

Yet the Centennial also introduced a wider public to "reform" ideas of design theorists such as the influential Charles Eastlake, who criticized the rococo carved rosewood furniture as well as the scenic and gaudily realistic wallpapers then in vogue. One facet of this call for simplicity was the Arts and Crafts aesthetic, which lasted well into the twentieth century. Craftsman homes stressed flat stylized designs in mellow, natural colors, and handcraftsmanship in what they considered "hon-

Left: *Art Deco interiors favored abstract geometric motifs, such as the sunrays on the headboard, and a bright palette that included leafy greens.*

Top: *Miami Art Deco depends on hot tropical tints of pink, turquoise, and yellow to fill the sleek angles and curves of this building.*

Color palette: *Dark moss green, slate gray, honey brown, and fuchsia of the Victorian era.*

Below: *Stark Modernist design theories of the early twentieth century still explored the power of color and pattern. In its bold form, this crescent couch is a fitting display for a geometric vintage fabric.*

Color palette: *Ocean blue, light turquoise, sunflower, and cream of the Aesthetic Movement.*

est" materials, such as fumed oak, leather, and hammered copper. Another reform approach was cottage furniture in wicker and white wood, painted with flowers and cushioned in chintz. Either approach could reflect a craze for "japanesque" fans and artworks, and aesthetic details in turquoise, cream, and gold.

In the last decade of the nineteenth century, colors in general were turning clearer and were used in fewer numbers with more emphasis on "harmony by analogy," a common Victorian design theory. The influential *Decoration of Houses* (1897) by Edith Wharton and Ogden Codman advocated a restrained French classicism in which "each room would speak with but one voice: It should contain one color, which at once and unmistakably asserts its prominence." Another bridge from

Victorian reform to the twentieth century was architect Frank Lloyd Wright's clean-lined, open-plan Prairie Style, with earthy hues derived from the landscape.

streamlined style

The Art Nouveau style flourished briefly around the turn of the century, with curvaceous lines and natural forms limned in glowing oranges and browns, with floral greens, yellows, and purples. In America, the style's prime showcase was Louis Comfort Tiffany's splendid metalwork and stained glass.

Such design currents fed into the streamlined yet colorful Art Deco designs of the 1920s and 1930s. In addition to clean black, white, and metallics, the palette tended toward offbeat hues, coral, apricot, tropical greens and pinks, and ocean blue. Colorful Bakelite plastics and sleek, vivid ceramics enlivened mundane household objects. "Pueblo Deco" evoked the southwestern Native American palette with the warmer off-whites of adobe and unbleached wool, accented in strong turquoise and rich orange.

Another movement vying for attention was Modern architecture, which aimed to shake interior design free of historic

Above: *Filmy fabrics and a misty scenic screen, all in cool pastels of the postwar years, give a dressing table 1940s glamour. Sharing the Hollywood ambiance are an offbeat ottoman, a necklace-like garland trim, and details in light-catching polished silver.*

Color palette: *Natural tan, plain oak, woodland moss, and leather brown of the Arts and Crafts movement.*

Above: *A kitchen recalls 1950s coziness, with knotty-pine wainscots, grass green doors, and a lipstick-bright enameled table of the era.*

Color palette: *Tropical coral, flamingo pink, black, and chrome of the Art Deco style.*

Opposite: *Here's an updated twist on a historic color: The trendy yellow-green on the walls of this Florida home was actually picked up from the 1950s vintage print.*

references and to create in bold planes of steel, glass, stone, and concrete, making the home a functional "machine for living." At the vanguard of Modernism was the Bahaus, a school of architecture and design founded in Germany in 1919. At its purest, Modernism strips the palette to white, black, metal, leather, and concrete, relieved with bright primaries. As the style was popularized, it warmed to neutrals and textures of wood, stone, and brick.

In the 1920s and 1930s, with new dyes that could color-match different materials and new brighter-white paints, monochromatic and white-on-white looks were chic in both fashion and interiors. Black-and-white color schemes gained glamour from a Hollywood association. The more subdued side of the Deco palette, emphasizing practical neutrals, browns, and midtones, dominated the Depression-era interiors.

Austerity continued during World War II, from 1939 to 1945, since consumer goods were in short supply and pigments and dyes were diverted to wartime uses. Manufacturers voluntarily limited color choices. Colors tended toward classic navy, gray-teal and other blues, cherry and coral reds, pearly grays, earthy browns, and olive drab in generally traditional interiors.

the postwar palette

At the close of World War II, decorator Dorothy Draper stated in *House Beautiful*: "The Drab Age is over. Color is coming into its own again." Once again, new technology paved the way. Young couples set up housekeeping in new suburbs and eagerly embraced Modernism minus the minimalism, with

design secret:
Play a saturated color, such as pumpkin or sepia, against ivory woodwork for an updated yet traditional look.

color lavished on new moldable laminates, easy-care fabrics, and intense synthetic dyes. The general postwar optimism might express itself in warm oranges, browns, and yellows, or a whole range of sweet, simple pastel blues, greens, and pinks. Sleeker Scandinavian-modern rooms might lean more toward neutrals and light woods.

Youthful attitudes also promoted the 1960s palette of psychedelic-bright accents and more complex

color mixes, such as orchid purple and copper yellow. The warmer range of dark yellow, orange, and olive green led into the earth-toned 1970s. Inspirations for the 1970s colors included rugged Southwestern looks, the stone blues and dark reds of country décor, and an interest in all things natural, coinciding with a crosscurrent of industrial high tech.

This muted decade set the stage for the explosion of color in the 1980s. Rich hues resurfaced with Memphis designs in hot pastels, "punk" aniline-dyed wools, or the lush pastel chintzes of English Country. Postmodernism sought to restore architecture's sense of history and decorative forms by rendering them in mint greens and sky blues, mauve pinks and gray. The resurgence of *trompe l'oeil*, sponging,

Right: *In a stark setting, the chrome weave of a 1960s "diamond chair" relieves flat tonal planes but doesn't compete with the vivid orange door.*

Color palette: *Autumnal orange, reddish brown, baby blue, and sweet pink from the Postwar palette.*

ragging, and other decorative painted finishes added color to interiors, along with textural interest and theatrical flair.

local color

"Everyone talks about regional differences dying out, but when you talk about color in the home, you're talking about local color," notes Margaret Walch. "In New York, you can even distinguish an East Side and West Side palette. People are more sophisticated about color, but even when they rebel, they're still very much rooted in the culture they were born in."

Regional palettes involve ethnic influences, historical and economic forces, the colors of the landscape, and most of all, the quality of light. The cool, thin light

Above: *United by a sunny yellow glow, this living room cuts loose from specific historic roots, pairing traditional and modernistic furniture and adding a personal touch with the line-up of hydrangea bouquets.*

Color palette: *Burnt orange and olive green of the 1970s, and orchid purple and copper yellow of the 1960s.*

of northern climates picks out the subtleties of muted tones, as demonstrated by the pastel yellow, gray, blue, and white of Sweden or Ireland's heathered wools. Such colors would be steamrollered by a full-bodied southern sun. In sunny regions, the palette tends toward saturated hues that look strong and glowing, as in vibrant Caribbean paintings; Provençal fabrics densely patterned with red, yellow, and blue; or Indian silks in spicy yellow and vermillion.

Above left: *The contrast of deep purple-blue against a golden yellow sharpens the sophisticated geometry of a New York City setting. Though arranged conventionally around a coffee table, the sculptural swept-back armchairs and low-slung, oversized ottomans take the room beyond the traditional.*

Left: *In a California home, the intense pastels popular on the West Coast are used to emphasize the lush curves of the Asian-influenced rattan furniture; the painting's bright, stylized poppies and the richly patterned pottery and tilework repeat the colors.*

"Colors have to fit the landscape," notes designer Lyn Peterson. "That's why you don't see a lot of barn red, maize yellow, and grass green in Florida, or beach colors in Pennsylvania. On a winter day in Michigan or Ohio, you appreciate subtle, warmer colors, which would just flatten right out in tropical light."

Arizona-based designer Sue Calvin concurs: "Some people think "Southwest" means pastel, but light tints just don't stand up to the intensity of our sunlight. The colors of Mexico and Spain are our inheritance, and they're hardly pastels." She cites instead rich reds and terra cottas, spicy yellows, blues and blue-greens, cooled with white. "In California, or even Colorado, the air is mistier and the sunlight is softer," she continues. "Pastels, particularly bright ones, work over there."

The Southeast traditionally inclines toward "pretty" light tints, which seem fresh in warm weather and hint at a certain classicism. Colors turn generally warmer and softer through the Midwest, perhaps influenced by understated Prairie Style designs. The Pacific Northwest, first settled by Yankees, long held onto a fairly conservative Northeast palette, though with an earthier cast.

Above: *A bathroom in a Pacific Northwest house captures a little of the clean austerity and restful neutral colors of Japanese design, a more recent color influence. The mood emerges in the finely crafted natural woods and the clean outlines, such as the shower dividers, which suggest shoji screens.*

Time-tested colors needn't fall into clichés. When designers Christopher Drake and Lee Bierly work with clients in Florida, they find that classic pumped-up pastels contrasted with white seem right amid the sunshine and tropical gardens. "But we're moving away from bleached-and-pickled furniture and floors," notes Drake. "People like the contrast and intensity of fine dark woods." With unexpected individual touches, you can put your own spin on traditional color combinations.

buying history

How deeply you indulge in vintage colors depends on your commitment, your goals, and your pocketbook. Many wallpaper and fabric companies offer documentary designs, which draw on historical patterns. Reproductions, in the strictest sense, recreate the original in design, color, and repeat size. Some very expensive products even reproduce the manufacturing methods, with block-printing, vegetable dyes, or hand silk-screening.

Historical societies and museums often enter into licensing agreements with large wallpaper and fabric firms, allowing them to produce collections based on their archives. Most manufacturers do some adapting to modern manufacturing and current tastes. Occasionally, the document might not be a wallpaper or fabric but a porcelain piece, clothing, or artwork. Regardless of the source, the design may be scaled up or down, simplified or filled out.

Above: *Subdued colors can play up shapes and textures. Traditional symmetry is the keynote here, with a dining area framed by a large fireplace and the living room by classic columns. The flow of creamy pastel tints points up such details as the taupe starfish motifs and the yellow scallop-edged table.*

Most importantly, it may be colored to suit contemporary tastes, providing the range of choices we expect.

Most paint companies offer collections of historic colors, a definition now broadened beyond the eighteenth century to the Victorian and Craftsman eras. Some collections are carefully based on the latest microanalysis of old finishes.

Yet many manufacturers keep the muted "Colonial" versions in the line-up, since they reflect the way we're used to seeing old houses. For a museum set-piece, historical accuracy dictates; in choosing colors for a home today, it merely suggests and inspires.

Above: *Similarly intense hues, trimming a New England seaside house, add unexpected but charming accents to the region's classic cedar shingle siding.*

Right: *A sunlit West Coast apartment gains a retro-charm from castoffs, reclaimed with fresh finishes. The various armchairs all harmonize with the 1930s-style sofa in gold-hued upholstery and vivid throw pillows.*

color theory and practice

color is merely a trick of the light. White light, which is made up of all the colors in the spectrum, jumbles together electromagnetic energy of varying wavelengths. A prism or misty sky can separate the tangle into an orderly rainbow, bracketed by violet-blue, with the shortest wavelengths, and red, with the longest. (Outside the visible spectrum are ultraviolet and infrared rays, with wavelengths too short and too long to be seen.) A different kind of sorting lets us perceive an object as colorful. As light strikes an apple or fabric swatch, the molecules of its pigments selectively absorb some wavelengths and reflect others back to our eyes. It is these rejected wavelengths that we perceive as the object's color.

The science of color is partly concerned with its precise measurement and the intricate chemistry of dyes and pigments. It also ventures into the more subjective realm of perception and psychology: exploring how colors relate to one another, how they affect the viewer, and how quantities, textures, and patterns alter the effects. A bit of color theory can provide a firmer foundation for the art of interior design.

turning to the color wheel

The interplay of light and color was explored by the seventeenth-century scientist Isaac Newton, who little reckoned that his abstractions would underpin the decorator's useful hands-on tool: the *color wheel*.

Previous page: *Glorious colors such as these are just wavelengths, until the eye and brain perceive them.*

Left top: *This setting mixes colors and patterns with gusto. Primary colors turn sophisticated with sunny stripes framing the red toile print.*

Left bottom: *Similarly, the brimming coffee table and pillow-piled couch layer exotic designs in a palette ranging from dark neutrals to hot pinks and yellows.*

The designer's wheel, which deals in pigments rather than light, pulls the spectrum into a circle to display the range of colors and clarify their relationships. Three equidistant slices of the pie are the pigment *primaries* of red, yellow, and blue, which can't be obtained from mixing other hues. Between each pair of primaries are the *secondary* colors—orange, green, and purple—created by mixing two primaries. Filling out the circle are *tertiary* hues—red-orange, yellow-orange, yellow-green, blue-green, blue-purple and red-purple—created by mixing a primary and secondary color. Though it's usually portrayed with discrete slices, the truest color wheel would be a continuum, as each color edges toward the next in almost imperceptible steps.

But the bold, clear color wheel is only part of the story. Each fine point along its spectrum can also mix with black to a range of darker *shades* or with white to create ever lighter *tints*. Mixing with lighter or darker grays creates muted dusty tones. Industrial color-specifying systems expand the color wheel into a three-dimensional cylinder, sphere, or tree to accommodate each color's light-to-dark and pure-to-muted range. Professionals can accurately pinpoint a color by three attributes:

❖ *Hue:* the designated color—e.g., a specific orange-red.

❖ *Value:* the lightness or darkness of a color, from a high-value baby tint to a low-value darkened shade. Adding white to a "normal" blue tints it to high-value baby blue; adding black shades the basic color down to a low-value navy.

❖ *Saturation, intensity,* or *chroma:* the purity or strength of the pigment. For example, a light blue could be a pure vivid pastel or a more muted grayed-down tone.

Even complex professional color-specifying systems don't come close to the four to ten million fine gradations of color theoretically perceptible to the human eye and the sixteen million distinguished by computers. And pigments for production runs of home furnishings are seldom as pure as abstract ideals. Yet a color wheel helps you think creatively about colors, their relationships, and their decorative potential. Just as a composer tinkers with musical notes on a staff, a designer

Below: *The color wheel's pure hues are only the beginning—each color can also mix with white into progressively lighter tints, left, or deepen with black into a range of darker shades, right. With their endless variety and their lower intensity, which makes them easy to live with, tints and shades are decorating staples.*

can begin to visualize harmonies, progressions, and intriguing touches of dissonance, with help from a color wheel.

how colors affect each other

The color wheel is commonly, and often loosely, divided between its yellow/orange/red side, generally seen as warm, lively, and stimulating, and the cooler blues, greens, and purples, considered more refreshing and restful.

Directly opposite any color on the wheel stands its strongest possible contrast, its *complement*. If you stare at an intense color, then look away, you may see an afterimage flash of the complementary hue as the eye's fatigued color receptors seek relief in an opposite sensation. Partly owing to this optical effect, com-

Above: *Complementary contrasts bring out the best in both colors, across a range of lighter and darker incarnations. For example, red and green might be Christmas-bright, or translate into this more sophisticated teaming of verde marble, rose chintz, and wine-tinted needlepoint rug with green and white bouquets.*

Below: *Terra cotta stucco glows even more warmly when it's accented with a lapis blue door. The surrounding bushes and trees in cool greens add another naturally appealing contrast.*

plementary pairs intensify each other. For a demonstration, think of the ebullience of red/green Christmas trimmings or purple/yellow pansies.

The complementary effect continues even if you vary the colors' tints and intensities. In fact, complements generally pair up more pleasingly if one is allowed to dominate and the other is muted or used as an accent. For example, bright blue might find a more subtle foil in deep terra cotta than in blazing orange. Juxtaposing complementary pairs of equal saturation in equal doses can confuse the eye with a jumpy, vibrating effect.

But all colors interact with each other. Our perceptions are relative, not absolute: The same light green wall seems pale behind an emerald sofa, warms up behind a blue sofa, and seems more intensely green behind a red one. Some rules of thumb:

❧ Complementary colors enhance each other.

❧ Colors that are not complements tend to make each other less "true." This also owes to the afterimage, which adds a tinge of the complementary color. Thus, a

clear red tends to take an orange cast against a blue background and looks more blueish against an orange background.

✤ While a contrast generally enriches a color, a darker companion in the same color family will mute it. For example, a crimson border will make a rose bedspread seem less saturated.

✤ Colors separated by black or white interact less than colors in direct juxtaposition.

✤ Black contrasts make colors seem brigher and more jewel-like. (Think of leaded stained glass or cloisonné enamelware.) Black throw pillows would make a midtone couch seem more pastel.

✤ White backgrounds intensify colors. Similarly, white accent pillows would deepen the upholstery's shade.

Below: *Colors of equal intensity tend to fall into harmony. A soft pastel ambiance holds together blue, pink, purple, green, and yellow—a complete spectrum—without discord in this sunny bedroom. The bed linens' brighter floral tosses in a needed accent.*

❖ Equally strong colors will to some degree cancel each other out and become harmonious. Thus several pastels can combine smoothly, as do a few smoky shades.

how colors affect us

Everyone agrees that color evokes an emotional response, but which colors, which emotions, and to what degree are up for debate. Sometimes the question is posed from the inside out: What do our chosen colors reveal about us? Surely an artist's palette as distinctive as Van Gogh's vibrant hues or Rembrandt's shadowy golden depths suggests an intense inner vision. Perhaps toddlers like bright colors because such hues reflect a child's straight-ahead energy. Rebellious teenagers may favor offbeat or even abrasive colors (which advertisers use to tap this market).

In the well-known Luscher psychological test, the subject repeatedly arranges color cards by preference, revealing strengths and deficits of personality. More popularly, thousands of Americans have undergone a personal color analysis, an enjoyable yet unscientific way to find "seasonal" hues to express their essence.

But more research has been done from the outside in, especially in Western industrialized society, as specialists in environmental design or functional color theory strive to determine how colors might make us feel better, work harder, learn more effectively, or open our purses to buy.

Many of the studies support the color wheel's warm/cool dichotomy. Warm colors tend to be invigorating, extroverted, and appetizing; hence their use in restaurants, from brash orange hamburger joints to elegant bistros dressed in wine-tinted velvet. In one study, children scored higher on IQ exams in rooms they saw as warm and "pretty" than in "ugly" brown rooms. But beware: Some studies indicated that red rooms heighten blood pressure and yellow rooms make the occupants more argumentative.

Cool colors tend to be more contemplative and introverted, especially in low-contrast schemes. Green sur-

Left: *Pale floors and walls visually expand a cozy breakfast corner. On the inside, the doors match the walls, for a unified sweep. But the brighter exterior paint job turns the open doors into charming accents on airy mornings.*

Above: *Color also sets a mood. In this study, a peaceful, contemplative spirit emerges from the dark natural woods, the exotic fabrics, and the deep reds of the Old World rugs. And what could be a more suitable background than the soft textures and colors of old books?*

roundings seem to speed time and diffuse tension, which inspires the theater's "green rooms" for jittery actors awaiting their cues. But such strategies can backfire: The pervasive use of green in schools and hospitals in decades past has prompted, in many viewers, a visceral dislike of the color's "institutional" shades.

All of which illustrates that color responses are subjective and changeable. Some people hold onto a favorite color through decades; others prefer variety. "Your life has probably changed in the last ten years," notes color expert Margaret Walch. "Colors and furnishings that made sense when the children were little or before you got married may lack relevancy now." And who doesn't boast a few color quirks—some inexplicable, others complete with a story: the green house from childhood, the horrible gray office, the amazing blue sea of a long-ago honeymoon.

We may be less aware of how our culture and era shape our color responses. In America and much of Europe, blue is a perennial favorite color, while red ranks first in other locales, such as Spain and Japan. Western brides dress in joyful white—a mourning color in some Far Eastern societies. Even within a culture, the accustomed palette changes. In the Victorian era, early Impressionist paintings shocked viewers, who saw them as garishly bright. Yet to our jaded eyes, the same paintings seem restfully pastel. Even closer to our own times, we might chuckle or wince at colors and combinations from a decorating guide dated 1955 or 1969—color that struck the readers of the day as perfectly keen or groovy. And a few decades hence, our own most stylish efforts may suffer a similar fate.

The pull of comfortable, traditional colors and the push for novel, newly fashionable choices have shaped the American palette since the nation's early days. But the home decorator can hold to one constant: Human beings seek variety in their surroundings. Light colors seem upbeat, clean, and lively but turn cold and monotonous if unrelieved. Dark colors are plush and enclosing but in excess can turn gloomy. Midtones are attractively comfortable, but a room decked completely in midtones can be dull. Bright, saturated hues are eye-catching accents, but uncomfortably demanding in quantity. In short, one could do worse than to follow the old decorating maxim "Something dark, something light, something dull, something bright."

strategic coloration

Bold colors, especially when warm, seem to advance. Just think of how azaleas and forsythias hold the foreground against an expanse of spring-green grass. Conversely, pale colors, particularly cool ones, appear to recede. Nothing seems more distant than the limit-

Above: *Many spaces could use a little visual reproportioning. In this boxy bedroom, painting one wall a bold blue and another a buttercup yellow makes the space seem less regular and more dynamic. Outlining the small, awkward window in high-contrast white transforms it into a focal point.*

Below: *A high, narrow kitchen was brought into balance by visually lowering the ceiling with black paint and pushing the walls back with white cabinets and appliances. The black-and-white note continues in old-fashioned mosaic floors and an iron-work bistro table. Egg yolk yellow, freely applied, adds some bounce.*

less blue sky; objects on the horizon, filtered through the interference of air and dust, seem grayer and cooler—the mountains really do have a "purple majesty."

"You can transform a really boring room with the right colors," notes California designer Lori Erenberg, "and make it sculptural and exotic or smooth and peaceful." In addition to using evocative hues, a skilled decorator uses colors—retreating or advancing, contrasting or harmonious—as strategic tools to reshape spatial perceptions. For such illusions, sometimes just a shift of a few tones is enough. If you feel the room is:

❖ *Cavernous*: Bring the walls in with warm, cozy colors, deep toned floors, and a darker ceiling, perhaps extending the ceiling's color several inches down the wall. For a more horizontal thrust, paint chair rails and baseboards in a contrasting color.

❖ *Claustrophobic*: Keep the eye moving with undisrupted planes of color and repeated patterns. Visually push the walls back with receding pastels or light neutrals, while raising the ceiling with still lighter tints or white. Choose neutrals or midtones underfoot, because oddly enough, a lighter-than-expected floor can seem obtru-

design secret:

Color can work magic on floors, too. To increase a sense of space in rooms with dark walls, paint or cover the floor in a mellow color.

sive. Moldings add character to cramped spaces but should be matching or low-contrast. Or consider making a virtue of the room's shortcomings by emphasizing the room's snugness with deep, enclosing tones.

❖ *Badly proportioned*: Ease a boxy space by emphasizing one wall with a darker hue and highlighting architectural features and windows. Minimize the "bowling alley" effect of a long narrow interior by painting the end walls in an advancing warm shade and breaking up the expanse with area rugs and furniture groupings.

❖ *Disjointed*: Blend various jogs, angles, and doors with a smooth wrap of a single color. Or in a large space, play up the architectural character with contrasts.

❖ *Overpacked*: Use the space-enhancing tips applicable to any small room, and paint built-ins to match. Furniture of modest scale, in light tints and soft patterns, will

Above: *The owners wanted to keep this large hallway generally free of furniture. To fill up the wide expanses, designers lavished on eye-catching color, with white-trimmed fuschia walls and area rugs in bright oversized patterns.*

seem less obtrusive, especially when blended into the background. Varied textures, including light-catching glossy finishes, enliven subtle colors.

❖ *Too sparse*: Compensate for a lack of furnishings by using rich colors and patterns to make the room seem more filled. "When you're moving into a new, bigger house," notes designer Gretchen Rhodes, "it won't look nearly so empty if you give all those walls a job to do, and finish them with some satisfying colors and details."

In furnishings, warm, bright colors are apt to make objects seem slightly larger, while cool, subdued tints tend to make a piece less imposing. A subtle pattern may soften the outlines, but strong designs make anything more conspicuous. With objects, spatial perception often hinges more on the degree of contrast with the background than on the colors themselves.

Use contrasts to underscore the room's fine features: Paint the ornate moldings in strong tones or pure white, or circle the

Left top: *Contrasts can be used strategically. The bright white fireplace makes the light gray wall seem darker and richer.*

Left bottom: *From inside a yellow bedroom, the stairwell's angles are played up by the space-enhancing blue and the dash of green on the half-wall.*

fireplace in elegant tilework. Conversely, to blend in a well-loved but bulky chair or an awkward radiator, camouflage it with a sweep of matching wall color.

textural notes

Textures and patterns also shape our perceptions of color. The same hue carries different connotation in sailcloth or silk, a nubby Berber rug, or a high-gloss laminate. Shiny textures soften outlines and increase illusions of space, with mirrors

Below: *Mirror-bright stainless steel catches the light, invigorating this kitchen with youthful energy and suggesting a nostalgic nod toward classic diners. (Such effects, however, often demand careful maintenance.) The glinting surfaces also pick up the floor's tropical blue.*

as perhaps the quintessential room-stretcher. Glossy surfaces make hues brighter and more light-filled. Thus satin pillows will outshine a "matching" twill sofa. Textural patterns, like damasks or satin stripes, that subtly play matte and shimmering surfaces, embody a sophisticated sense of tradition. Whether in a satin-and-gilt French rococo chair or a chrome-and-buffed leather Modern version, glossy surfaces tend to have a refined, manufactured sensibility.

Cozier matte finishes absorb light to make objects seem more substantial and colors more subdued. Plush fabrics, such as velvets and Jacquard weaves, can have sophisticated appeal. But rugged textures, such as brick, wicker, canvas, wools, and rough pine, often exude a natural, country-style setting.

Like every aspect of decorating, textures involve a balancing act. A multicolored room might be brought together by using fabrics of similar texture and weight, while a more monochromatic scheme demands tactile variety. To give a room a distinctive character, you may let one type of texture predominate, as in a den with deep carpets and tapestry couches, or a dining room in gleaming rosewood and wallpaper flecked with gold. But the right contrast—bright brass end tables in the den or

design secret:

Too many colors can be too confusing. Limit your selection to four colors—or patterns—in a room. The design will still have visual variety, but it won't be overwhelmingly busy.

velvet curtains in the dining room—can make the scheme more intriguing.

seeing a pattern

Pattern also affects our color perceptions. While it's possible to imaginatively play them against their conventions, many evocative patterns—tartans, paisleys, floral chintzes, intricate Provençal cottons, country calicos, breezy ginghams, dense ethnic weaves, pop-art abstracts—conjure up specific traditions and eras, which in turn suggest appropriate color ranges.

Pattern makes any color, even the softest pastel, more eye-catching. Big, boldly tinted, high-contrast, densely packed patterns appear to advance, while mild, small-scale, low-contrast designs are more retiring, particularly if they have plenty of open, neutral ground. In general, patterns should be in scale with the room; a minisprig or a small stripe gets lost in a large space, and a big pattern is hard to appreciate close up.

Try to view a pattern at the distance and angle it would take in the room: Lay flooring samples underfoot, and step back from the propped-open wallpaper book. Drape the window fabrics in folds to see if the design and colors still read well. A large, bold pattern requires some preplanning on the specific wall or furniture piece so those palm fronds or birds-of-paradise won't be awkwardly cut off in mid-motif.

Above: *Though this master bedroom mixes a variety of patterns—a geometric quilt, floral bed linens, ticking stripe draperies, and a dotted-swiss skirt—they all share an informal character, and a recurring emphasis on pretty shades of blue.*

A miniprint that contrasts strongly with its background, particularly if widely spaced on the field, can give a busy, "dotted" look on a large expanse. A lower-contrast version, however, can be a subtle visual texture that nicely disguises less-than-perfect walls. Small patterns can have unexpected repercussions in your color schemes—a crisp little red-and-white check may come across as an unintended pink.

Mixing patterns can be intimidating, in part because it's subject to experimentation, judgment, and "eye." Responding to this fear, manufacturers provide an abundance of coordinated mix-and-match wallcovering and fabric collections, available through wallpaper books and in-store design services. Such collections, engineered by professionals, can save you a lot of legwork and still leave scope for your own input.

The secret to mixing patterns is to provide links of scale, motifs, and colors. The regularity of checks, stripes, textural looks, and geometrics, particularly if small-scale and low-contrast, tends to make them easy-to-mix "neutral" patterns. A small-scale floral can play off a ticking stripe, while a cabbage-rose chintz may require a bolder stripe as a same-scale foil. You may choose to use the same or similar patterns in varying sizes or develop a theme by focusing on florals, geometrics, or ethnic prints.

But the most effective link is shared colors or a similar level of intensity between the prints. A solid-color companion that pulls out a hue shared by two prints provides another connection. Exact matches are the backbone of manufacturers' co-

Above: *A Western theme draws together the vivid reds and turquoise blues of this living room, and harmonizes the strong patterns of Indian blankets, woven rugs, calicos, cowhide, and the folk-painted chair. The white-washed brick walls and raised hearth share the rugged unifying concept, serving as a cooling background.*

ordinated collections. But to arrive at your own personal mix, you can take the principle more loosely. "People get very focused on 'matching,'" says designer Lyn Peterson. "Then when the light changes, or the items age a bit, the colors are never going to match again. It's better to think about a choice being in a family of colors and deciding what looks great together, rather than seeking exact matches."

practical goals

Beware of letting theoretical design goals overrule common sense. "If you have kids, you don't want white sofas and white walls," explains designer Pia Ledy. "Instead, you want a bit of pattern and rich color to camouflage all that living. You don't do an interior to preserve it, you have to live in it."

Shiny surfaces, while glamorous and visually light, require upkeep; dark lacquers and high-gloss cabinets reveal fingerprints and dust more readily than matte finishes. Light fabrics or carpets will show soil (though protective finishes can help), and heavily dyed brights or darks are more prone to fading.

Design aims need to be filtered through your own color preferences. If you love dark colors, you may prefer a room that looks a bit smaller to one that is bland. When you can satisfy both the practical and aesthetic concerns, the results will wear well, in every sense of the phrase.

Above: In a bevy of Provençal-style cottons, a pillow-heaped sofa appears a cohesive whole because the intricate patterns are of similar scale, in hues of equal intensity. Simple planked walls in white provide a visual breathing space.

light up your color ideas

Without the subtle interplay of matter with light, color would not exist. The old saying "At night, all cats are gray" holds true—the level of illumination and the mix of wavelengths in the light, natural and artificial, affect which colors are reflected back. Cool, blueish light, for instance, intensifies blue and green tones while underplaying warmer reds and yellows. Warm light does the reverse, muddying blues and greens while pumping up the intensity of the spectrum's warmer hues. Early in the nineteenth century, colors had to be bright to come across in dim candlelight. (It takes about 120 candles to equal the glow of one bright light bulb.) By the turn of the century, the trend toward subtler hues was due partly to the availability of gas and electric lights.

Above: *Natural light, while tipping toward the warm side, is perceived by the eye as the desired norm.*

Previous page: *Pure white teamed with a pastel hue, such as this airy tint of green, strengthens the available sunlight.*

Thus lighting shouldn't be an afterthought to the finished room. Because it creates the colors and shapes the room's mood and spatial impressions, lighting should be integrally planned. You may want to visit a "lighting laboratory" showroom to assess new products and talk with a staff consultant. For an extensive project, you might hire an independent lighting designer or an architect or interior designer trained in this specialty.

starting with nature

To the human eye, the desirable norm is sunlight. Current architectural trends and energy-efficient windows provide sun-swept interiors to indulge this craving. Part of sunlight's appeal is its variety. Travelers often sense the differences—the clear illumination on a cloudless mountaintop, the misty softness of a bayou morning, the intensity of light on a tropical beach. Such distinctions help foster regional palettes that look good in the characteristic light. Yet even stay-at-homes experience sunlight's changeability between a cool rainy day, a clear winter afternoon, and a full summer blaze. Noonday sunlight is the most spectrally balanced, while red and yellow wavelengths dominate as the afternoon wears on into evening.

Similarly, the room's exposure will likely influence color choices. North-facing rooms get little direct sun. Artists often prefer the cool northern light,

reflected off the blue sky, for judging colors. But a homeowner might want to visually warm such a room with reds, oranges, and yellows, at least as generous accents. A slightly warm scheme might also enhance an easterly room's tentative morning light. But in a room facing south that gets maximum exposure throughout the year, or a west-facing room that confronts intense rays on warm afternoons, you may opt to turn down the heat with cooling blues, greens, or purples.

Even by day, however, most interiors require at least some manufactured lighting. You'll need to consider three types:

❧ *General lighting* to provide a comfortable ambient glow.

❧ *Task lighting* to add brighter illumination for a specific activity such as reading, crafts, or cooking.

❧ *Accent lights* for decorative flourishes, either subtle or dramatic. These fixtures might include pinpoint spots on paintings or sculptures, uplights to enhance archi-

Above (left to right):
Two views of the same kitchen illustrate how varying the light levels, with sunshine from arched windows and with the artificial glow of unobtrusive fixtures, can gray-down or brighten the same medium blue walls.

tectural details, or soft wall washers to make the colors pop.

Personal preferences to some extent dictate lighting levels—what seems bright and upbeat to one person seems overbearing to another. An older person's eyes generally require brighter illumination, with a minimum of glare and shadows, for comfortable working conditions.

Fairly high-key lighting enlivens colors, making them brighter and richer. You may be surprised at how new wallcoverings or carpeting can change a room's general lighting level, as dark or matte surfaces soak up the illumination.

gauging the glow

Effective lighting design involves a balance in the layering of light and plays with illumination of varying intensities. Bright overall lighting can seem flat and harsh; contrasts give depth and interest to the room. High contrasts, however, require the eye to constantly readjust, which can be tiring. (You may sense this watching TV in a completely darkened room.) Lighting professionals often start by planning the room's task lighting, then adding the ambient glow to smooth the transition between these stronger pools. Accent lighting to play up decorative focal points is the icing on the cake.

One measure of light is its intensity or brightness, measured in *lumens* for a nondirectional glow or in *candela* for a directed beam of task light. Lumens per

Above: *Accent lighting draws the eye to artwork, and brings out its details and rich colors.*

Right: *Unobtrusive ceiling fixtures and a rustic chandelier create this room's ambient glow. Yet reading lamps alongside the seating, and accent spots on artworks, layer on depth and variety.*

watt (LPW) designates how much light is provided for the watts used—a measure of energy efficiency. That's usually about as much information as is found on the basic grocery-store light-bulb package.

But a more specialized lighting store, catalog, or home center expands the specifications on the bulbs (called *lamps* by lighting professionals). One criterion is the light's color, stated as its Kelvin temperature (K rating) or Correlated Color Temperature (CCT). Color temperature has nothing to do with the actual temperature of the bulb or the light—it designates the temperature to which a certain metal in a laboratory test was heated to release a glow of a particular hue. The Kelvin scale runs from reddish candlelight, at around 1,500K, up to 9,000K, just past the rating for a northern blue sky. Summer sunlight is a little short of 5,500K, and standard incandescent bulbs span 2,000K to 3,000K, with higher-wattage bulbs

Left top: *Here, incandescent light enhances the warmth of the red walls.*

Left bottom: *Cooler colors, such as lavender-blue and gray-green wall stripes, are washed out by the glow of a lamp.*

producing whiter light. Thus, paradoxically, the higher the Kelvin temperature, the cooler the light's color. For home lighting, the recommended range runs from 3,000K to 3,500K.

While the Kelvin temperature tells what the light looks like, another rating, the Color Rendition Index (CRI), or R factor, indicates how accurately a light source will show colors. Idealized daylight has an R factor of 100. For artificial lighting, the closer the number approaches 100, the more accurate the rendering. A range from 75 to 100 is desirable for interiors.

bulb basics

To create the right light, you'll need to choose the right bulbs. *Incandescent* bulbs contain a burning filament that emits light as a by-product of heat. *Fluorescent* bulbs are coated inside with a material that glows when struck by electrons from the charged gas vapor inside.

Incandescent bulbs are the least expensive and most commonly used variety. Their soft, warm tint lends a

Right: *For the best results, lighting should be planned in advance. Here, the recessed lighting is purposely focused on conversational areas in this living room. A floor lamp provides backup lighting for reading.*

design secret:

To see how light affects a wall color, place a painted sample board in the room, and then check it both day and night.

pleasing glow that flatters skin tones and plays up warm reds and yellows in your decorating. But the generally yellowish light will tone down greens and blues and will mute purple, yellow's complement. Incandescent's strongest disadvantage is that the bulbs are relatively short-lived and inefficient, using about 90 percent of the energy consumed to produce heat rather than light.

Halogen bulbs, a special category of incandescents, offer greater efficiency and longevity to compensate for their higher initial cost. They burn hotter and thus produce a whiter, brighter light with good color rendition. The clarity of the light makes halogen a common choice for accent lamps. Halogen bulbs with screw-in bases can replace a standard light bulb in some fixtures. Reflector bulbs have a shiny interior coating to direct light in a focused beam. Halogens also come in a variety of tubular shapes designed for specific fixtures. Standing torchières with tube-shaped halogen bulbs provide an attractive diffused lighting, but their high temperatures can create a fire hazard if they're unstable or come in contact with combustible materials, such as curtains.

With *low-voltage halogen* lamps, a transformer, either separately installed or within the fixture itself, steps down the standard 120-volt line electricity to 12 volts. These bright, compact, energy-efficient bulbs are favorites for accent lighting because they unobtrusively tuck into tight quarters and shallow recessed fixtures. Some of the fixtures include snap-in gels to add decorative touches of color to the accent beam.

Above: *A decorative as well as functional element, the frosted glass shade of an elegant bronze torchière casts an amiable glow in this Midwestern living room.*

Incandescent lights readily adapt to dimmer switches, which let you shift the lighting to mood and activity. Standard incandescents edge toward red as they're dimmed, while halogens take on a yellow glow.

the flowering of fluorescent

Fluorescent lamps provide more light worldwide than any other source. Compared with incandescents, they provide two to five times as much light per watt, particularly if used for long stretches of time. But fluorescents suffer an image problem, stemming from their use in cold, shadowless industrial settings and from the unnatural spectral distribution and poor color rendition of the earlier standard fluorescent. A classic "cool white" fluorescent intensifies blues and greens but robs yellows and reds of their visual warmth and skin tones of any healthy glow. Similarly, furnishings bought under a store's fluorescent lights may undergo a sea change under the warmer lamps at home.

But fluorescents have taken on a whole new look. "Cool white is no longer the only option," points out architect and designer Robert Orr. "Just as you pick out colors of paint, you can choose and manipulate colors of light. By checking the specifications, you can find fluorescents that match the color of incandescents." Energy codes in certain locales require installing efficient

Below: *With a flexible lighting plan, you can shift the illumination toward the theatrical for the proper occasion. Jazzy, sharply defined pools of light dramatize this room's height and architectural details.*

fluorescents in kitchens and baths, a development creating a demand for more appealing products. For a warmer light, look for bulbs with a color temperature rating from 3,000K to 3,500K. More expensive, rare-earth phosphor coatings achieve higher color-rendition ratings. "Full-spectrum" bulbs emulate the wavelength distribution of sunlight.

Straight fluorescent tubes are the most common shape, though certain fixtures require U-shaped and circular lamps. Slim-lined miniature units are also favorites for under-cabinet task lighting. Perhaps the most useful version is the compact fluorescent, with the tubes looped into a standard screw-in base and sometimes encased in a smooth cover. A compact fluorescent can replace a standard incandescent light bulb—and for its higher purchase price, save you an estimated $50 in electricity and replacements over its

Below: *Warm, even-handed lighting, with small spots of brighter illumination, plays up a kitchen's subtle woods and gleaming black columns.*

long life. To keep color rendition uniform across a room, use the same types of bulbs from the same manufacturer, particularly in matched fixtures, such as wall sconces flanking a sofa.

decorative potential

Though lighting plans should be part of the room's groundwork, the fixtures themselves can also be delightfully colorful finishing accents. Overhead lighting is often designed to be unobtrusive, but wall sconces and table and floor lamps draw the eye with their glow and put the spotlight on their own textures, shapes, and colors.

Torchière floor lamps throw light upward to reflect off the ceiling into a general glow, but only if the ceiling color is white or pale—a strong color will affect the quality of the light. A table lamp with an opaque shade directs light more sharply up and down; a rose-tinted or gilded interior is an old trick for giving the light a flattering cast. With translucent shades, a lamp provides more ambient light; the shade should be white or cream-colored to avoid tinting its glow. Since lamps and sconces are relatively small and come in a variety of motifs, richly colorful ones can effectively punctuate a color scheme, while illuminating the overall design.

Left: *The unusual mix of vibrant red-and-yellow upholstery on antique furniture calls for lighting fixtures that won't fade into the background These star-shaped sconces fit the bill.*

selecting your color palette

hen you first start thinking about decorating, you can flirt with any number of colors. But eventually you must settle down with a color scheme—a combination of a chosen few. What guides this process? Where can one even begin? Strict rules about combining colors are hard to come by because each hue takes an infinite number of guises. Deciding if red will go with blue in your house, for example, depends on whether you're talking about crimson and robin's egg or brick and indigo. A red, blue, and yellow scheme might be beachhouse bright primaries or transmuted to a serene rose, cobalt, and cream for an elegant dining room. It is natural to be hesitant about using color. But with practice and some guidelines, the process becomes easier.

Just as in any recipe, a color scheme comprises both the ingredients and the amounts—a teaspoon of salt adds savor to a stew, while a cupful makes it unpalatable. As design writer Barbara Mayer points out, a gray room with hot red accents and a red room with touches of gray technically have the same scheme—to very different effect.

While it's hardly an unbreakable rule, in general, the stronger a color, the less of it is used. Bright color can be wearing in too great a quantity. A dollop of saturated red equals in visual weight a whole wall of cotton-candy pink. "There are no ugly colors, just ugly proportions," notes designer and color consultant Catherine Stein. "Colors that might clash in equal doses might seem merely lively if one is a small accent to the other."

Another decision is the number of colors. Particularly when you're just gaining confidence in your decorating, it may be helpful to limit your palette in a room to two to three principal colors, perhaps in different shades and tints, combined as necessary with white, black, or neutrals. But don't be evenhanded with them: Colors are generally more pleasing in unequal amounts. A room split

Previous page: *Trim, tulips, and towels in peachy pink warms up a bathroom of cool, water-colored glass tile and chrome.*

Right: *Yellow, pink, and green, though widely separated on the color wheel, can harmonize elegantly in their softer incarnations. Dark woods and white trim add definition to this color-rich living room.*

evenly between two colors can seem jumbled because the eye doesn't know where to look. Letting a particular color dominate provides clarity and focus.

looking with
new eyes

Design professionals generally make their final decisions, including more risky ones, with hands-on samples, intuition, and an "eye"—an ability to visualize specific colors and fresh combinations. An inborn gift to some extent, an eye for color can also be a developed skill.

To sharpen your color sense, try to appreciate and analyze the hues all around you. Out your window, observe different greens or browns in the landscape or the changes in the blue sky. In a garden, decide which flowers look right together. How many colors lurk within a single bloom? Even on a routine grocery trip, slow down to really see how lemons differ in color from yellow peppers and which look better against the eggplants.

Right (top to bottom): *For a sense of flow, this bedroom's elements draw their colors from the headboard's strong floral chintz. A kitchen tableau hints at purple's possibilities, from flowery pastel mauve to the purple-black of eggplant.*

Clockwise (left to right): *Favorite objects of porcelain, art, and antiques, looked at with a fresh, appreciative eye, may inspire a room's color combinations. The contrast of deep blue on the polka dot chaise against the clear white and sunny yellow of the wood-work and walls give this bedroom its verve. If a room focuses on a colorful collection, such as these stacks of vintage Fiestaware in a red cabinet, keep the surrounding hues in a more muted supporting role.*

How do grocery packages use color to manipulate your response? When you enter a fabric store, what hues immediately draw your eye? How did you choose and combine your clothing this morning?

"You can get color ideas everywhere," says designer and colorist Lori Erenberg. "Look at new books and magazines, including ones from Europe, because their colors are different." Vintage books and magazines can be equally eye-opening; antiques, old linens, even classic car colors can suggest less mainstream choices. "On a walk, I can see subtle shades in weeds and bushes, stones, sand, and the ocean," she continues. "Look at the latest couture fashions to see what's going on there—use everything around you as a palette."

Most of all, analyze interiors—a theater lobby, a dentist's office, a friend's house, or the examples brimming from magazines and books. Which color schemes do you find appealing—or appalling? What ideas would you steal or adapt?

"Often, as a starting point, we'll ask a client to go through a stack of magazines and rip out anything that instantly appeals to them," says designer Christopher Drake. "Then we get together with the pile in the center of the table and talk over the pictures to find some common threads." Is one color represented over and over? Are the contrasts bold or muted? Are the rooms densely patterned or serene, traditional or funky, darkly snug or brightly sociable?

Designers frequently use this tear-and-talk method as a starting point. By giving concrete examples of hard-to-define concepts, it ensures that everyone is talking the same language. Otherwise, one person's cheerful could be another's gaudy; what one person finds tranquil might strike the other as humdrum. If these people happen to be married to each other, finding common definitions is the first decorating hurdle.

color wheel concepts

A professional designer might play with schemes by considering some time-honored configurations on the color wheel. An *analogous* scheme involves neighboring colors that share an underlying hue. *Complementary* schemes pair up colors directly opposite each other, such as orange and blue, while a double complementary involves an additional set of opposites, such as a blue-purple and a yellow-orange.

A *split complementary* joins a hue with the two colors flanking its complement for a somewhat subtler contrast. For example, instead of teaming

design secret:

If your favorite color is too intense for walls, use a "dirtier" version— add black or raw umber to make a darker, more livable shade.

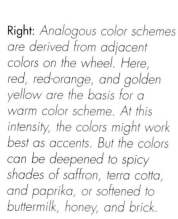

Right: *Analogous color schemes are derived from adjacent colors on the wheel. Here, red, red-orange, and golden yellow are the basis for a warm color scheme. At this intensity, the colors might work best as accents. But the colors can be deepened to spicy shades of saffron, terra cotta, and paprika, or softened to buttermilk, honey, and brick.*

yellow with purple, the mix shifts to yellow with blue-purple and red-purple.

A *triad* involves three colors equally spaced around the wheel, such as red/yellow/blue or green/purple/orange, while four equidistant colors, such as yellow-orange/green/blue-purple/red, form a *tetrad*.

If such combinations sound a bit Technicolor, remember that colors in interiors are rarely undiluted. Thus yellow might be cream, blue-purple a dark eggplant, and orange-red a muted terra cotta or whisper-pale peach. With less jargon, such combinations fall into two basic camps:

❖ *harmonious*, or *analogous*, schemes, derived from nearby colors on the wheel—less than halfway around; and

Above: *A shared hint of yellow brings together a scheme joining warm terra cotta and Old World olive. Four patterns—a miniprint, exotic stripe, plaid, and flame stitch—coordinate in this room because of similar scale and color intensity.*

Above: *Various tints of one color unify this indoor/outdoor setting. A apple blossom pink bedroom opens onto a porch painted peachy pink with white trim. The adjoining master suite continues the pale pink theme.*

❖ *contrasting,* or *complementary,* schemes, involving directly opposite slices of the pie.

The sense of sequence and flow between related colors tends to make harmonious schemes peaceful and relaxing. The narrower the segment of the wheel, the smoother the flow. Color experts Annie Sloan and Kate Gwynn note that hues between any two primaries on the color wheel—for example, blue-red/purple/purple-blue—are very harmonious. But a sequence that "spans a primary," such as a yellow-green/yellow/yellow-orange or a blue-green/blue/blue-purple, is potentially more discordant and requires more careful planning.

At their broadest, the colors in a harmonious scheme might range over the whole warm or cool side of the wheel. Perhaps the ultimate in harmony is a monochromatic scheme that rests on one hue, spun out into tints and shades from dark to light and from intense to "stepped down." Neutrals are often added freely. While such rooms have an inherent space-maximizing unity, they risk looking contrived or monotonous unless cleverly varied with inviting textures and tonal contrasts. A predominantly monochromatic scheme might, in the end, require a few bracing accents from the wheel's other side.

That approach is the heart of contrasting schemes, which tend to be livelier, with a pleasing balance of warm and cool. Technically, to maintain a

Right: *Colors that span a primary, such as yellow-orange, yellow, yellow-green, may require careful coordination in a room scheme because the underlying, unifying color—in this case, yellow—is less obvious. Allowing one color to dominate and weaving the other two in as accents could enhance the harmony.*

Left: *Colors that fall between two primaries are very harmonious, making it easier to create a pleasing color scheme. Unlike colors that span a primary, there is a smooth transition between related colors. Vivid hues, such as these purples and warm blues with a hint of red, are usually toned down to less intense tints when used in interiors.*

true complement, as one color shifts toward the cooler side, the other warms up. For example, a cooler blue-green opposes a warmer red-orange. But the power of contrast is felt with a choice anywhere along the opposite half of the wheel. Blue's direct complement, for instance, is orange, but it is just as successfully paired with yellow or red, two hues that flank orange on the color wheel. Strong contrasts may need tempering with plenty of neutral ground. A contrasting scheme can also be stepped down to darker shades or turned toward pastels: Red and green could be more livable as rose and sage, apple blossom and mint, or maroon and forest green.

the importance of tone

A successful color scheme also involves the right harmonies or contrasts of tone. Strictly speaking, a *tone* is a grayed-down color, such as rose or terra cotta. But more loosely, tone refers to a color's density and light reflectance. Tone involves two factors: the *value*, or the amount of white and/or black in the mix, and the *saturation*, or the color's purity and strength. A gray scale from white to black is the clearest example of tonal range. But each color also spans a range encompassing dense jewel tones and dark shades, mid-tones and powder-soft clear or grayed pastels.

Above: *Though the furnishings are sedately traditional, the contrasts— warm burnt orange and spring green drapes, pale textiles and dark woods— give this living room a striking originality. Throw pillows in deeper shades, as well as a collection of china and greenery, help anchor the color scheme.*

To judge tone, reduce the colors to shades of gray. How would the room come across in a black-and-white photograph? Squinting at the space or the product samples through almost-closed eyes mutes the colors and leaves only contrasts, which are easier to evaluate. If the hues seem to merge, they're of similar tones.

Colors of similar tones tend to be harmonious, even if the hues are different. In Victorian times, polychrome wallpapers employed as many as twenty colors, all rich and muted enough to harmonize. The same unity prevails in a dark, intricate Oriental rug, a multipastel nursery, or a pile of intensely bright Indian sari fabrics. Thus a room of many colors can be brought together by keeping to similar tones.

However, one can have too much harmony in a room. Pale tints all around can turn flavorless; dark-on-dark can veer from cozy into overpowering; and wall-to-wall midtones can be dull and lifeless. If something seems to be missing from your scheme, it might be a problem of tone—even a red, green, and yellow room might seem a little flat if the colors are all of equal intensity.

Such a room can be sparked with some darker accents or high-value brights. Or if the room is all harsh contrasts of light and dark, adding midtones will smooth the transitions. Remember that wood has its own

Left: *Complementary colors lay opposite each other on the color wheel. The combination of red and green can be toned down to sage and rose for a springlike scheme or deepened to cranberry and evergreen for a more rugged ambiance.*

Below: *Used in skillful pro-portions, a basic primary scheme of blue, yellow, and red takes on a friendly sophistication. Repeating a pattern—in this case, the check pillows and the border on the watercolor artwork—visually coordi-nates a color scheme.*

tonal range from pale ash to gleaming mahogany. As with color, tone is rela-tive: What might seem a mellow midrange hue in one setting could be an effectively dark accent against creamy expanses in another location.

real-life roots

Despite what's been said so far, real-life color schemes seldom spring from theorizing. Often they hang on a peg more personal and concrete—an exist-ing element, a fabric or wallpaper pattern that speaks to you across a crowded store, a piece of artwork, a geographical or historical inspi-ration, or simply a favorite color. Each of these common starting points have their own strategies:

An existing element: Few deco-rating projects offer the luxury of start-ing from scratch. Perhaps you have a handsome brick fireplace, a magnifi-cent needlepoint rug, or an expen-sive sofa that will star in the new room. Make it stand out strongly with a neutral backdrop, or surround it with softer complementary colors to push it forward. Pick up its colors for other elements in order to refer every-thing back to this focal point.

In a less happy scenario, you may be stuck with an element— an almost-new carpet or sturdy bathroom tilework—in a color

design secret:

Highlight beautiful architectural elements such as crown molding with warm hues. Use cool, low-contrast colors, however, to make unattractive features less prominent.

you loathe. One approach is concealment: The unloved carpet can be mostly obscured with an area rug. Hide or distract attention from the tile with an opaque shower curtain, a washable wall-to-wall rug, and big fluffy towels spread on racks. Ceramic tile can be refinished with special paint or, if you're more ambitious, professionally reporcelained or tiled right over with thin-set mortar.

You can also work with an undesirable hue. A very dated tile might initiate a humorous "retro" bath. Offsetting the color with lots of white might freshen it up, but that approach can backfire by emphasizing the color itself. Instead, team it with an analogous hue you particularly like. A classic solution is to find a strong print that lightly incorporates a bit of given color, then turn to the print's other hues for the remainder of the décor.

A patterned wallpaper or fabric, or distinctive artwork: A pattern that you like is a time-proven underpinning for a color scheme. In the design

Clockwise (left to right): *A completely neutral background spotlights each added element, such as this verdigris-and-gilt mirror; however, such strict color schemes, while dramatic, are difficult to maintain in a much-used room. Four distinct colors, widely spaced on the color wheel, abstractly constitute a tetrad; translated to a mellowed range of primaries, the combination flows briskly through an upper floor of bedrooms. Favorite colors can resonate from room to room: The rich, darkened red dominating one room becomes a small accent accessorizing the room across the hall.*

you get a preview of how the colors, chosen by professionals, will interplay, with clues on how much of each to use. While using the print lavishly on walls, furniture, or window treatments, you can pull out its background color or lighter tints for the walls, its darker tone for the floor, and its "top-notes" for accents. More dramatically, you can turn your color scheme toward less expected proportions for dark, glossy walls or a pale carpet.

You're not bound strictly to the color value in the patterned fabric. Try using a lighter or darker one, but don't tip the color toward another hue. To find an accurate color value, match one of the pattern colors to a paint strip, and then choose one of the lighter or darker versions on the strip. "A color has many tributaries and offshoots," notes designer Lyn Peterson, "and they're all there for you to use."

A geographical or historical inspiration: A house with strong period or regional ties may prompt you to research appropriate colors, though maybe more for the flavor than for strict accuracy. The farther afield the inspiration, the more you may need to adapt the palette: The colors of a tropical vacation might look gaudy in a city apartment; Tuscany's Old World colors may look drab without the timeworn textures; the summery pastel palette of the West Coast may seem chilly on an East Coast winter day.

Left: *Split-complementary color schemes consist of a hue and two colors flanking its complement. Here, blue is paired with orange-yellow and yellow-green, a vibrant combination with a tropical air. When tinted to light blue, orange blossom, and celadon, this trio takes on a softer sophistication but still retains its lively impact.*

The natural surroundings may shape the choices. "Georgia has a lovely mild climate, but it's not overly sunny," says color consultant Rebecca Ewing, "so colors that are slightly toned down tend to look good here." California-based designer Lori Erenberg based one house on the off-greens and creamy tans of the eucalyptus and acorn-laden oak trees outside. To layer personality on a room, she favors historic colors— "historic for California, at least," she jokes, citing "old Hollywood" colors, mellow Craftsman bungalow tones, or classic Spanish hues.

A favorite color: If you favor a particular color, it can spark a decorating scheme as you spin it into its light and dark shades, play it against neutrals, and pick an enlivening contrast or two from the opposite side of the wheel.

Left: *Color intensifies in quantities, so the broad planes of walls and draperies tend to be subdued. Here, the lightened green and rose tints team up in a serene bedroom. The floral pattern of the bed curtains is repeated on the rug.*

design secret:

Create a focal point in a room by painting one wall a different color. It can be a contrasting color for a bold effect or a deeper shade of the original color for a subtle emphasis.

Looking in your closet can also suggest potential decorating colors. "If clients can't tell me their favorite color, I take a look at what they're wearing as a start," says Drake.

The test isn't foolproof, however: Many people happily wear more intense colors than they'd be willing to live with day to day. "I encourage clients to have a palette for their wardrobe and one for their home, and that they be different," says Ewing. "Who wants to blend in with the sofa?" Another of her suggestions: "Make the colors in your home very different from those in your working environment," she advises. "It's hard enough to get a reprieve from work, and color can help with the transition."

Choosing the springboard for your design and zeroing in on the right colors is only the beginning. The hands-on work begins as you tailor your preliminary ideas to the particular setting, as seen in the next chapter.

refining your color plans

however far you reach for fresh color inspirations, decorating ideas eventually must be grounded in the demands of the actual room. "Even when you discuss colors early on," notes architect and designer Robert Orr, "you can't make final decisions until you can stand in the space and see the quality of the light and how the rooms relate to each other." And, he continues, "When you start to bring in real-life products, you have to deal with how the colors change each other." Thus the hues in your mind's eye may need to be pumped up or toned down, once you start to collect samples and view them on-site. Fresh ideas still emerge at the hands-on stage— maybe you'll see a need for a brighter accent or a softer background to emphasize a favorite feature.

Even more important is tailoring the room to the occupants and their purposes. "As a designer, I can't swoop in and say 'This room just must be red' or 'This color is all the rage,'" says designer Gretchen Rhodes. "The home has to be not about me or the latest fashion but about the people who live there. When we work out a palette that's personal to them, that's when they love the results."

a sense of proportion

Just as an artist initially sketches a picture's broad outlines, the interior designer usually thinks first about the room's "body tones"—the large background planes. Floors and ceilings represent the largest unbroken expanses. Most modern-day ceilings have little impact, but whatever you choose underfoot is conspicuous, since eyes tend to rest there, and standard down-lights keep the area well lit.

Even in fairly neutral tones, stone, tile, and wood provide rich, textural character. Wall-to-wall carpeting, which is sound-absorbing and space-enhancing, may entail a more definite color scheme decision because it

Previous page: *Warm accents—hot pink trim on ticking stripe slipcovers and a yellow pillow—keep the blue-and-green scheme of this country room from being too cool.*

Left: *This gracious living room epitomizes traditional decorating advice. The darkest hue, royal blue, was chosen for the Oriental rug; the walls were painted in a midtone of cheerful yellow, leading up to an expansive white ceiling.*

Below: *Deep-blue walls are a striking choice for an island kitchen. White woodwork, cabinetry, and counter-tops keep the richly colored walls from darkening the windowless room.*

is not easily changed. Area rugs, which are handily movable and cleanable, offer opportunities to insert striking hues in exotic ethnic patterns, bold modern motifs, or homey braided or hooked textures. In America's early days, precious Oriental rugs were often draped over tables or walls to show them off better.

Ceilings and walls add up to about two-thirds of the room's color. Because bright hues in such quantity may be overwhelming, subdued colors, if not neutrals, are typically used. "It's hard sometimes to persuade people to put *any* color on their walls," notes designer Pia Ledy. "White or beige can be beautiful. But when you use color, people respond. That's when you get comments about how fun or charming a room feels." But putting a definite color or pattern on the walls can be intimidating because it so clearly sets a mood or a theme. To apply even a muted hue, you need a fairly good idea of the room's contents.

Because it frames a room with personality, an attractive wallpaper, chosen early in the decorating process, can be a particularly effective organizing principle. Paint is more adaptable. It's easier to find or custom-mix a paint color that goes with a particular wallpaper or fabric than vice versa. With a painted finish, you can decide initially on blue

or green but hold off on the exact choice until the other furnishings are selected.

Traditional decorating advice puts the darkest tone underfoot to anchor the room, the lightest on the ceiling, and midtones in between for walls and furnishings. While hardly inviolate, this guideline still offers practical advantages: an easy-to-keep floor, a midrange hue that you won't tire of quickly for the bulk of the room, and a light-reflecting ceiling.

Walls in dark, dense colors, such as hunter green or eggplant, have an opulence, particularly in large, high-ceilinged spaces relieved with large doors, windows, and pale moldings. If the furnishings are a bit sparse or undistinguished, a rich background can help fill the space and satisfy the eye. But make sure you want the sense of enclosure that dark walls lend. More practically, a white wall reflects up to eighty percent of the light, a dark blue wall less than twenty percent. Thus dark backgrounds demand higher-key lighting. Glossy surfaces will make the walls more reflective but will also reveal any surface imperfections.

Certain visual tricks may help blur the room's exact dimensions. In one small study, designer Gretchen Rhodes glazed the walls a rich bittersweet orange and painted the ceiling white, slightly tinted in the same color. She then extended the ceiling color down the wall

Above: *Integrate an accent color by repeating it more than once. Here, purple-blue echoes in the drapes, pillows, throw, and even the candlestick.*

Left: *Muted tones—sage, taupe, and dusty blue—are the unifying link between an entry and parlor.*

Far left: *Instead of visually lowering this vaulted ceiling with a dark color, the designers washed it in pastel blue to accentuate its airy heights.*

about nine inches, defining the edge with a fine-beaded molding. "It suggests the ceiling has that much more expanse," she explains, "so we could have the drama of a rich color without making the room feel closed in."

The final seasonings in the scheme are the enlivening accents, provided by pillows, lamps, pieces of artwork, towels, molding, and collectibles. For a particularly strong accent, complement the dominant color with a saturated choice from the wheel's other side. Harmonious accents, in vivid or darker shades, are less disruptive but still effective. If you're not up for a complete redecoration, some strategic new accents can freshen up a room by fetching out a hint of color in a subdued background or emphasizing a certain hue in a print

When you bring in an accent color, use it with confidence and apply it more than once. Bright yellow curtain tiebacks, used alone, may look random. But add yellow throw pillows and a yellow motif in the rug, and they become part of a unified whole.

working with samples

It's hard to jump-start a large decorating project when each decision depends on the rest. Sometimes an impulse purchase sends the whole in unwanted directions; more often, the number of choices seems overwhelming. But by gathering

Above: *To balance this triadic color scheme, strong expanses of blue and yellow meet with an equally vivid hot pink armchair in this children's room. Furniture in a dark walnut finish is a restful counterpoint to the intense colors.*

samples for each element, you can work on assembling the big picture and test ideas before committing.

Actual product samples are needed to visualize and fine-tune the design because a manufacturer's pigments and dyes are less pure than theoretical colors. The same hue reads differently in different materials, whether linen, chintz, laminate, or wool carpeting. Because colors are changed by their companion hues and by the room's lighting, experimenting with samples on-site constitutes an important trial run. Colors are so subtle, and color memory so notoriously poor, that even professionals try never to match from memory.

Color tends to intensify in large quantities. Many a homeowner has been shocked by the change from paint chip to a full wall. If you're con-

Right (top): *These disparate fabrics—the cabbage rose print, yellow-and-cream stripe, and fuchsia solid—were composed on a presentation board before they were arranged in the sitting room.*

Right (bottom): *Testing swatches of the blue pillows against the diamond-decked cushions and the neutral sofa ensured a good mix.*

sidering a rich background color, at least cut up a handful of paint strips to tape together a larger swatch. Better still, buy a pint of the paint and brush it onto a large piece of primed plywood or poster board and look at it in the room. Try to see the sample in isolation, since a pure white wall in the background can make the color seem unrealistically bright. The larger sample may suggest the color be muted slightly for the intended effect.

Similarly, you should work with the largest possible samples of fabric, wallcoverings, and flooring, which may be available for a returnable deposit or a small fee. If necessary, buy a yard of fabric. View these samples at the intended distance and angle—draping the fabric over furniture or gathering it in folds by the window—to see whether a delicate pattern fades out or an exuberant design grows overpowering. Place a carpet piece on the floor, and move it from spot to spot to catch the varying light.

Designers often assemble a *presentation board* of the room's paints, fabrics, floorings, and the accents (represented by appropriately colored bits of paint chips, ribbons, or swatches). A presentation board can be any white-colored 8½ by 11 inch (or larger) surface. Foam-core board, available at art or hobby stores, is best. The samples approximate the proportions of the finished room: roughly two-thirds designated to walls and ceiling and the remaining third divided between floors and furnishings. Use rubber cement to attach the samples to the board.

Below: *To determine whether your color scheme will work, collect samples of the fabrics, floorcovering, wallpaper, and paint under consideration. Arrange the pieces on a presentation board in roughly the same proportions that they'll be used. Bring the board into the room, and judge the assembled samples by natural and artificial light.*

Even if you don't compose a formal presentation, at least bring the samples all together in the intended space and examine them for several days under the room's natural and artificial light. Does your enthusiasm stay high? Do you need to expand or edit the range of color and textures?

site-specific planning

Color schemes aren't one-size-fits-all. The most successful ones are custom-tailored for a particular space. In your clear-eyed assessment of your needs, here are some aspects to consider:

Physical space. Consider not just whether the room is large or small, but how the dimensions drive the plans. In a big room, would you rather scale down for a more intimate mood or emphasize the room's lofty spaciousness? In tight quarters, will you pull out every space-enhancing trick or bring on rich, deep colors to create a cozy "jewel box"? Is the space disjointed by doorways, windows, and jogs, asking to be unified in a smooth sweep of color? Or is it a bland box that calls for detail? There may be elements you want to downplay. What are the room's fine features—the ready-made focal points?

Above: *The handsome plaid upholstery of this study echoes the blue of the marble fireplace surround. The palette of deep wood tones and vivid cobalt blues reinforces the "gentlemen's club" atmosphere.*

Is the room located in a suburban ranch, a town house, a clean-lined apartment, a country house, or a beach bungalow? The color scheme may reflect a distinctive architectural period or regional character. You don't have to listen to the house's suggestions—an East Coast apartment can have a Southwest flavor or a country house some big-city slickness—but playing against type takes more design ingenuity.

Also consider the prevailing climate. If you face chilly, rainy winters, consider the psychological warmth of sunshiny tints and deep textures. In hot regions, smooth surfaces and light backgrounds seem particularly fresh and cool.

Natural light. As noted in Chapter 3, the room's orientation can influence the palette, depending on whether you're trying to tone down or maximize the available light. In a true sun room, dark or bright textiles, which are prone to fading, might be reserved for easily changed accents. Before tailoring a room for sunshine, make sure the artificial lighting also flatters the selection, as many homes are used more during evening hours.

Lifestyle concerns. Will the room be a high-traffic space, requiring washable, forgiving surfaces and colors? A space reserved for company occasions might be jazzed up with glamorous, less practical choices. What activities take place in the room—reading, crafts, watching TV, or conversation? Is it a family space, ready to accommodate romping toddlers, or will it mainly be a province of sedate grown-ups? Do family members have any strong color opinion you'd like to accommodate?

Will you spend long hours in the room or brief periods? Rooms you

pass through briefly can usually carry off more dramatic colors and patterns than rooms where you linger.

Atmosphere. What sort of mood would you like the room to project? Lighthearted? Elegant? Tranquil? Stylish? Homey? "Color is often the mood setter," notes Orr. "So it's helpful to ask, 'Is this a room where we'll be paying bills or sipping margaritas?'" The room's purpose often prompts the color choices. You might, for example, lean toward an invigorating tint for a home office, while a peaceful, low-key shade may better suit a bedroom. The atmosphere should also relate to the room's purpose. You may, for example, need an energetic color for a home office, but a peaceful low-key color may suit a bedroom better.

Above: *A lack of natural lighting was the primary problem in this apartment hallway. To enhance the the available artificial light, a glowing yellow covers the walls and ceiling.*

Left: *While rich reds and browns might seem too enclosing for a basement, this walk-out lower level has a sunny wall of windows (not shown) that makes the intense hues seem cozily sophisticated.*

a room-by-room tour

Specific rooms in the house introduce their own color-scheme criteria:

Entry halls are generally small, yet they bear the big job of providing a welcome and an introduction to the house beyond. If it's a main entrance with heavy traffic, wet boots, schoolbags, and swinging umbrellas, think twice about delicate or pastel finishes. In this short-stay room, you can consider more theatrical treatments: The limited wall space might be the place to experiment with special painted effects. Be wary of dark treatments, however, which can seem cavelike if you enter from a sunny day. Delineate any steps, jogs, or changes in level with color contrasts for safety.

Below: *Red beadboard, which might seem too warm in this kitchen, is tempered by off-white surfaces and a dark green border. A fruit motif on the tiles ties the colors together.*

Because the furniture is usually minimal, walls and floors set the scheme. A hall is often an effective display area for colorful artwork; flowers and plants can supply natural hues. An entry that opens into several rooms requires visual links to each.

Living rooms come in different styles. Some are company parlors that showcase luxurious finishes and striking color schemes. Others, particularly in older homes, emphasize *living* and need a family-room approach, perhaps with extra storage and a touch more formality to present a company face. In many Cape Cod or ranch-style houses, the front door opens directly in, adding an entry hall's traffic.

Several comfortable, movable chairs may prove more versatile than one big sofa, and color can unify a diverse collection of furniture. In a house with a strong period character, the living room is usually closely attuned to the theme.

Family rooms appeared in post-World War II houses as multi-purpose spaces, a spirit generally reflected in the decorating. Neutrals and pastels can smooth together a room that bustles with books, games, papers, projects, displayed crafts, and media equipment. Avoid large, distracting patterns on walls behind a TV screen or displayed collections.

Furnishings with rich, tightly woven textures, matte surfaces, midtones, and darker neutrals will minimize dirt and wear, while bright accents can lend the proper cheeriness. A family room is gen-

Left: *Forest green walls might be too dark for bedrooms or living rooms, but in this dining room, it's the perfect backdrop for golden pine furniture.*

erally linked to the kitchen with a color connection as well.

Kitchens tend to be individualistic. Some are country-cluttered; others are streamlined and no-nonsense. If yours is a sociable family space with heavy-duty cooking, lean toward practical midtone and neutral colors that wear well rather than dramatic effects. Such rooms are less likely to date quickly, since kitchen fashions swing periodically from very light to dark and cozy. Kitchens rarely seem big enough for all their functions, so light colors have an advantage, though pure white can require more cleaning. A fairly dark, neutral floor with some pattern will simplify housekeeping.

Cooking and washing up are hot activities, so a dominating yellow or red might feel overwarm. Be wary, however, of giving the room a strong greenish or blueish cast, which is unflattering to food or skin tones. If your dining area is an eat-in corner of a kitchen or living room, it needs to be planned in concert with the adjoining space, though perhaps differentiated with a shift in palette. Blue accents in the kitchen, for example, might deepen to a navy in the dining area.

design secret:

When working with a color you can't change—pink tile, for instance—introduce accessories in a harmonizing color to diffuse the effect.

Separate *dining rooms*, notes designer Lyn Peterson, "can be a bit 'over the top' in the decorating, since you use them for fairly short, festive periods of time." Consider warm, appetizing colors, which also tend to look good by low light, in classic patterns or glazed finishes. Variable lighting with dimmers, candles, and accent lights adds extra sparkle. If you have a favorite restaurant, you might draw inspiration from there. Dining rooms that serve for everyday meals, or double as a home office, homework space, or craft area, demand sturdier materials and a quieter approach.

Be sure the color scheme incorporates the various linens, mats, and dinnerware, which hold the foreground when the crowd gathers at the table. "People don't realize that when they choose their china," adds Peterson, "they're picking the color of the dining room for the next few decades."

Bedrooms are private spaces, where individual personalities can have free rein. Easy, peaceful colors are often preferred, though some people like a deep, dark atmosphere. Make sure all choices look good by artificial light. If the background is kept fairly neutral, a new coordinated set of bed linens and curtains can periodically transform the room. Sheets can also provide reasonably priced yardage for coordinated home-sewing projects.

Matte textures are cozier. Some homeowners like to shift the bedroom with the seasons, stripping it down to a few cool patterns and

Below: *Layers of texture, from muslin bed curtains to an embroidered spread to a tapestry pillow, create the romantic opulence of this Old World bedroom.*

Below: *A subtle pink scheme suits the dual nature of a guest room, which doubles as the owners' quiet corner for household paper-work and correspon-dence. The color exudes hospitality yet is low-key enough to make an undistracting home office.*

window blinds in summer, then layering it with a pile of dark-colored woolly throws, heavy drapes, and scatter rugs in the colder months.

Children's bedrooms generally serve as playrooms and workrooms as well. If you want to indulge yourself in a pretty nursery, choose colors and materials that will adapt or change easily. (The baby won't care.) A toddler will be thrilled to help pick colors, and a school-age child will likely expect to. Working together on a room can be a creative project; with an older child, consider invigorating a paint job with stamps and stencils. Teenagers may want to put their own stamp on their bedrooms with offbeat color combi-nations that assert their individuality.

Home offices range from a bedroom alcove for organizing the family bookkeeping to a dedicated suite of rooms for a home-based business. If your business involves visits from clients, the home office generally has to exude reassuring professionalism, with a "serious" low-key color scheme. A businesslike, pared-down atmosphere in neutral colors also helps make the transition from home to work environment. If it's strictly a behind-the-scenes work-place, you can revel in working among your favorite colors.

Light colors visually expand the well-filled office and foster the fairly bright light levels recommend-ed for close work. Harsh white, however, can be glaring.

Bathrooms generally pack a lot of standardized equipment into a tight space. Neutral fixtures and tile allow a lavish hand with colorful wallpaper, towels, rugs, and accessories. If you're short of storage, open shelves of stacked towels can add bright accents. The more adventurous may consider decorative tiles and fixtures in a rainbow of choices, often correlated between different manufacturers. Dark glossy surfaces, unless well-rinsed, readily show soapy streaks. Deep colors also compromise the bright lighting required in a room where you shave.

Unless you're fond of long, leisurely soaks, bathrooms are short-stay spaces where the decorating can have a bit more scope. Psychologically, warm colors may make the room more comfortable and flattering to skin tones. Since the wall space is small, the bath can be another handy place to experiment with special painted finishes.

whole-house scheming

If you're faced with decorating several rooms at once, it's easy to get caught up in each one's individual demands and overlook the unity of the whole. But a small home or one with an open floor plan takes on a

space-enhancing flow when each space resonates with the next. "A house is a community of rooms," points out designer Lyn Peterson. "Some are neighboring communities; some are more distant." A sense of connection is usually most important in the house's more communal and public side—the entry; the living, dining, and family rooms; and the kitchen. The bedrooms, a home office, or library may be more stand-alone.

Color is perhaps the most versatile link. One common solution is a light, neutral background running from room to room, ready to team up with various stronger colors.

Above: *Both this living room and dining room share a common color theme—russet red, golden yellow, and leaf green. A fruit motif on the fabrics and artwork also unifies the décor.*

Left: *A collage of blue-green tile is a refreshing dash of color in a serene bathroom. White fixtures and neutral-colored floor tiles are easier to maintain and are less likely to become dated.*

Repeated flooring provides a firm connection: A hardwood floor in the living room, a patterned hallway rug, and a matte-textured vinyl kitchen floor could all share a mellow tan tone. Sometimes a single color provides the link; each of the fairly neutral rooms might incorporate touches of strong red or brilliant blue. Coordinated wallpaper and fabric collections offer charming possibilities for whole-house scheming. For example, a hallway's bright floral could lead into a moiré-textured living room, while the library uses the same floral in an opposite coloration.

In another approach, a few chosen colors run through the whole house in different proportions and intensities. For example, in a house focused on green, blue, and gold, green may dominate the living room and be just a wallpaper border and cabinet knobs in the kitchen. Such unity also lets you shift items between rooms more easily. After all, explains designer Lyn Peterson, "A house can't be all one note, but it should be the same song."

a walk on the warm side

the glow of a steady fire, the buttery warmth of afternoon sunlight, the romantic red rose, all embody the stimulating, warming, engaging nature of reds and yellows. Especially when undiluted, these warm hues seem to advance toward the viewer, making space seem cozily enclosed or pushing an element into the foreground. This effect may derive partly from red and yellow's longer wavelengths, which focus deep within the eye. But it probably owes as much to the colors' tactile, here-and-now association with fire, sunlight, and flowers. Warm colors energize a room's atmosphere. Reds are festive and lively; yellows glow with cheer. Either shade is uplifting yet serene when softened to an appealing pastel.

Previous page: *Orange, darkened to terra cotta, has an Old World richness.*

Below: *A medley of warm tints conveys this home's hospitality, from the petal pink entry to the living room in fresh yellow and the dining room in dramatic red.*

Color palette: *Pure red, spicy orange-red, maroon, and bright raspberry.*

Warm colors can be zestful and enlivening, just the thing for an upbeat playroom or hospitable dining area or to warm up a chilly north-facing family room. In excess, warm hues can turn brash or overwhelming; bright, undiluted reds and yellows are often reserved for powerful punctuation. But each warm hue also spans an array of congenial tints and shades, such as pink and orange.

red: exuberant and versatile

Red is a primary color in several senses: This elemental color of blood and fire is a favorite with very young children. In scientific studies, red rooms actually make the occupants feel warmer—a point to consider if you're turning down the thermostat. The color's powerful associations differ between cultures. In the Western world, red has racy, rebel-

lious connotations, but in many Eastern cultures, a bride wears red to reflect her new creative role. Red draws your eye, whether to stop signs, fire trucks, or a flash of a cardinal's wings in winter trees. Because pure red is so dominating, it can jazz up a bland color scheme or direct attention to such highlights as a sculptural scarlet leather chair.

Red has long been a sought-after color. Red ocher clays, often brought from great distances, figured in the cave paintings and funeral rites of prehistory. Crimson dyes obtained from crushed kermes insects were treasured in ancient Greece; cochineal beetles were equally valued by the Aztecs. In America's early days, imported Indian calicos dyed with madder-plant extracts, fine toile prints in rich beet-root shades, and treasured Oriental rugs glowed in candlelit interiors. Plush, dark russets and burgundies were favorites in the mid-Victorian palette. Brighter reds are a folk art perennial, as seen in the painted furniture of the Pennsylvania Dutch.

Since strong red in room-sized doses may be too demanding, its vitality often comes to interiors in less aggressive guises—darkened to urbane maroon or brick or tempered with blue to a raspberry. (See color palette on page 104.) Soft yet rich

Left: *Red glows with a special richness by natural light. In this sunny room, the pale woods, creamy floors and ceiling, and touches of stone blue all temper the red expanses.*

Clockwise (left to right): *Red is a dining room favorite, but it is also a fresh contrast with a white sofa. Russet and ocher spread warmth in a dining room. Pink is an almost-neutral background in a cozy bedroom.*

Right: *Pink set against opulent dark wood, chintzes, and artwork can be unexpectedly formal when paired with a black-and-white checkerboard floor.*

Color palette: *Cotton-candy pink, passionate hot pink, apple blossom, and warm tea rose.*

reds can be especially hospitable in entry halls and dining rooms.

Red absorbs a lot of light. A library with crimson wallpaper will be cozy on winter evenings but will demand extra task lighting for comfortable reading. Red glows by sunlight, especially the warmer afternoon rays. It's similarly flattered by incandescent lighting but is washed out by the blue-green cast of standard fluorescents.

pink: feminine and flattering

One can talk of light greens and pale blues, yet red tinted with white seems to merit its own designation: pink, ranging from a hot pink to a tender apple blossom. (See color palette, right.) Sweet pastel tints generally connote youthfully feminine trimmings (though Victorians reversed our pink/blue notions, assigning the more "vital" pink to rugged baby boys).

Flamingo pink, the delight of the Miami Deco style, was a tropical twist on the color. Elsa Schiaparelli, a 1930s Italian designer, turned heads with "shocking pink," a special hot pink that isn't as surprising today. Bouncy pastel pinks were popular in the 1950s, suggesting the era's youthful exuberance.

But pink can extend far past its stereotypes, as a versatile range of choices that add a hint of red's warmth without its assertiveness. As a background, whisper-pale warm pink can add a flattering glow yet remain a space-enhancing neutral. Deep shades of coral or rose can embody a tropical atmosphere or turn formal against vivid gilt and dark wood details. Clear, blued hot pinks and fuchsia might invigorate a more modern setting, relieved with plenty of white.

Pink extudes a relaxed charm that easily blends with other colors and harmonizes various patterns and textures. Like red, pink is enhanced by juxtapositions with complementary greens, as demonstrated by vibrant leafy rose chintzes. Paired with blue, a pink may seem sweeter as the

Clockwise (left to right): *Lively pink walls, with dashes of pink and red throughout the furnishings, create a garden-fresh atmosphere; the screen provides green contrasts. Pink can be fun and off-beat, adding a distinctive bounce to a breakfast nook's hand-painted personality. Pale pink is a warm yet low-key background a home office.*

overall effect is cooled down. Coral pinks will look equally warm teamed with buttery yellows or neutrals. Pink also may be a perfect foil for strong no-color schemes: A wall painted candy pink will show off a black-and-white checkerboard floor to its advantage.

yellow: luminous and lighthearted

Yellow layers a sunshiny warmth on the chilliest of rooms. Deep, saturated yellow is the most eye-catching color. This quality, so advantageous for taxicabs, can disrupt a scheme unless balanced

against plenty of neutral ground. A pale buttermilk tint—a warmer alternative to white—provides an appealing yet unobtrusive luminescence as a background color. This tactic can enhance the natural light or create the illusion of sunlit space. By that same logic, however, a strong yellow may seem overpowering when a room bakes in the afternoon sun.

Yellow is not a dense color; adding white quickly lightens it to a cream, and a green or brownish tinge emerges as it darkens. Yet this range displays yellow in many moods, from a pale primrose to a

Right: *Sunshiny warmth, inherent in yellow, loosens up a living room's formal symmetry. White moldings and bright dashes of cool blue provide the counterpoint.*

Color palette: *Earthy olive, clear lemon, soft sherbert yellow, and bright golden yellow.*

Left: *Yellow in a soft buttery shade glows as an unobtrusive background for a diverse collection of strong artwork and rustic antiques. The imaginative, free-form floor design repeats the wall color.*

full-bodied daffodil hue, from warm curry to darker, more dignified incarnations. These mustard and olive tones embody an Old World sophistication, though they can be changeable in artificial light; yellows with a smack of blue come across as an acidic, clear lemon, which has a fresh, youthful feeling. (See color palette on page 110.) A touch of red turns yellow toward warm floral tints of buttercups and sunflowers or golden, spicy shades of curry and turmeric. Gold and gilt details can be considered as yellow in a luxurious mode.

Yellow has been used since antiquity in earthy tints derived from ocher clays, embellishing Italian villas, African huts, or tinting early American whitewashes and paints. This dulled hue still exudes an antique charm as an excellent background to brighter accents. In the early nineteenth century, chrome yellow introduced a sharper, clearer hue, favored in the era's neoclassical homes. Yellow in a formal mode, paired with white woodwork, was used lavishly in sun-starved English manor houses. Its more relaxed

design secret:

Create a dramatic backdrop for china collections by painting a vibrant color, such as raspberry, on the back wall of a cabinet.

country mood is seen in Provençal fabrics with tight patterns of saturated yellow balanced against equally intense red and blue.

Yellow is enriched by incandescent light, though very pale tones can look washed out in the generally yellowish glow. Since luminous yellow is greatly affected by the ambient light, you may want to test a particular shade in quantity before committing to it. Its light-catching qualities and soft richness can bring special depth to decorative painted effects and overglazes. Because of yellow's luminance and delicate interaction with light, textures are particularly important. Bright or pastel yellows seem particularly airy in silks or damasks, while soft, earthier shades are cozier in velvety paint or woolen weaves.

Soft ocher and olive are restful backgrounds. They look more neutral against clearer strong brights, while cool companions emphasize their warmth. Yellow's direct complement is purple, but it finds a fresh contrast and

Above left: *Bright yellow, the most eye-catching color, turns a tile wall into a focal point. Such bold colors are often used effectively in short-stay rooms such as baths.*

Above right: *The luminance of yellow translates well to decorative painted finishes, such as the sponged bedroom walls and the lively painted mural in the adjoining bath.*

Right: *As it darkens, yellow takes on an olive cast. That deepened tone lends an earthy serenity to this country living room.*

a sense of balance in all shades of blue or with gray for a cooler pairing. Brisk lemony yellows contrast richly with warmer, red-tinged blues. Deep floral yellows can seem especially golden when teamed with rich reds and deep clear blues.

orange: earthy and energetic

Between red and yellow runs a useful range of warm orange tones, from blazing bright hues to sweet melon and peach tints to darker autumnal shades and rugged terra cottas. (See color palette, below.) The mellower versions have a long tradition in interiors. Inspired by the soft, earth-pigment-based tints of antiquity, clear apricot tones were a favorite in eighteenth-

Above left: *Pale peach is a decorating perennial because it is a warm hue that isn't too bold. The contrast of pure white plays up the light tint.*

Left: *Orange darkened to terra cotta has an Old World richness that brings out the glow of woods and works well in contrast with greens and blues.*

Color palette: *Warm desert orange, spicy dark orange, zesty tangerine, and delicate orange blossom.*

century parlors. Richer burnt orange was a favorite in Art Nouveau palettes, and offbeat coral shades in Art Deco accessories. Vibrant orange hues, popular from the 1950s into the 1960s, also provide part of the warmth of Southwestern schemes. Pure saturated orange is a high-energy, eye-catching color, as shown by its role in life vests, warning signs, and casual restaurants. Like red, it's a bold, advancing hue not to be used lightly. It can make an bracing accent or underpin an active, playful space or a short-stay room where drama is desired.

Orange's softer side includes a bevy of livable, mixable colors, ranging from almost-yellow marmalade hues to deep rosy shades of peach, very flattering to skin tones and natural light. At their palest, such tints merely add an unobtrusive glow. Deepened to rich terra cotta shades, orange has a comfortable solidity.

Orange's warm composition might require some cooling contrasts, so consider accents from the family of blues and greens. Gray might be another less-expected choice. The whole orange range blends well with wood, bringing out its warmth.

Above: *This room offers a sophisticated play of orange's warm tonal range, from soft melon tints to deep burnt orange walls. White woodwork tempers the intensity of the wall color.*

cool it down with color

an endless, cloudless sky, deep grassy meadows, the purple haze of distant vistas all embody the spacious serenity of the color spectrum's cooler side, where greens edge into blues, which stray into blued purples. Such colors can take the edge off a sun-baked room, making it seem more an oasis. And what could better create an outdoor feeling within walls? Blues and greens, linked in daily experience with landscapes and limitless sky, tend to recede from view. In their paler incarnations, cool surroundings can push back the visual boundaries of a room. Conversely, a piece of furniture or an architectural feature finished in a cool, harmonious hue may seem less obtrusive. In general, cool colors are considered tranquil and soothing.

Previous page: *A verdigris wall creates a luminous backdrop for a collection of black-and-white photography.*

Color palette: *Tropical water blue, pale icy blue, weathered blue, and bright Empire blue.*

Above: *Red, white, and blue—a homespun country combination—turns streamlined in this sunswept open floor plan. Strategic dashes of red and expanses of wood counterpoise the freshness of blue.*

But don't stereotype cool colors: A brilliant turquoise or brisk kelly green will certainly be more assertive than a soft rose tint, even if the other is technically "hotter." And some mellow shades of blue with red undertones or greens that lean toward yellow can be quite cozy.

blue: fresh and harmonious

A majority of Americans and western Europeans tag blue as their favorite color, probably for its connotations of harmony and serenity. But blue is a color with endless moods: sleek navy, summery azure, vivid cobalt, or a comfortable midtone. (See color palette, left.) Blue can be a delicate robin's egg tint or a blazing lapis. No wonder, as the writer Colette wrote, "There are connoisseurs of blue, just as there are connoisseurs of wines."

Nature is prodigal with blue in sea, sky, and flowers, but a clear hue was difficult for long-ago craftspeople to reproduce. Ceramics have vivid traditions in the color: Blue-and-white porcelains from China, the rage of seventeenth- and eighteenth-

Right: *Vistas of sea or sky may inspire a blue color scheme. Here, the vivid lapis blue linens played against pure white reflect the seascape views.*

Below: *Muted shades of blue convey a graceful serenity in a traditional room. The rich color of the upper walls is echoed in the table linens and rug.*

century Europe and America, inspired European production of similarly embellished majolica and delftware in shades of blue from light to dark. Indigo, a source of a rich blue fabric dye, was transplanted from India to Europe to the Caribbean. In the 1740s, Eliza Lucas Pinckney, a South Carolina planter's seventeen-year-old daughter, started experimenting with indigo cultivation and promoted a new cash crop for the Colonies.

Muted gray-blues and skylike tints decked both walls and furniture in Colonial America and remained a long-lasting country favorite. By the eighteenth century, green-tinged Prussian blue, cobalt blue, and artificial ultramarine often enlivened the fashionable walls of drawing rooms and dining rooms in more intense shades.

design secret:
Instead of white on ceilings, try misty blue or pale green to draw eyes upward. Then select a harmonizing wall color.

Blue is the essence of cool. Liberally used, it can temper a glaringly sunny room, though the same décor might seem icy in a space lacking natural light. Blue's inherent sense of depth lends spaciousness, especially in its lightest skylike tints.

The color remains "true blue" across its many tints and shades, which tend to mix well with each other. Yet blue's strong personality gains charm from the right contrasts. White is the crisp, clean foil employed in country ginghams, formal toiles, ticking stripes, or classic chinawares; yellow or red is a warmer partner. Blue often works well with yellow of the same intensity, whether both are pastel or saturated. Dark blues can seem formal and opulent, detailed in gold or cream, or warmer when teamed with wood tones. Country blues grayed down to stonelike shades can be dull unless sparked by brighter contrasts, such as calico red, or freshening white.

The complementary orange might play a better supporting role if softened to peach or deepened to dark amber. "Blue with green should never be seen" is an old but unfounded saying, since the two have an inherent har-

Clockwise (left to right): *Blue's cool depths and the sunny luminance of yellow add a pleasing balance to a dining room's lively celestial theme. Time-tested blue-and-white runs through several exotic prints draping this breakfast corner. A study in blue: Time has weathered the cupboard and floor boards of a mud room into a soft denim tint.*

Below: *Against clean white, this grassy green becomes even more refreshing. Gold and mirrors add extra glamour without disrupting the bold, simple color scheme.*

Color palette: *Fresh kelly green, bright yellow-green, subdued mint green, and bluegrass green.*

mony, time-tested in nature. Between blue and green you also find beautifully ambiguous blends—teal, turquoise, aqua—which often look best with warm accents.

green: natural and revitalizing

Green is nature's favorite color, the color of living things. As a mix of blue and yellow, green's balance of warm and cool is easy on the eye, with a laid-back, space-enhancing tendency to recede from view. Its dual nature encompasses refreshing greens that lean toward blue, as well as warmer, more yellowed hues. Though technically a secondary hue, green is a "psychological primary" that most people view as basic and irreducible.

A landscape showcases the color's subtleties, running through yellowy mosses, fresh grass, shady oaks, silvery birches, and dense firs. (See color palette, left.) Nature mixes greens freely, and so can the decorator, though certain blue-greens and yellow-greens may fight if used in equal quantities. Nature's own colors can be part of your decorating if the design directs the eye toward a verdant view.

Deep forest shades handsomely play off-white, cream, or wood, which help provide the ample light needed to show off this dense color. Bright acidic greens are bold and modern, with an attitude that is youthfully iconoclastic. Intriguingly ambiguous blue-greens, in all their variety, can vary with the light to look more blue by sunshine and more green by incandescents. Like blue, cool green gains focus from the right contrasts. Complementary reds or rich pinks intensify its vibrancy.

Several minerals and clays yield the natural green pigments used in early paints and washes. In the late 1700s, bright apple green was fashionable, as well as paler celadon tints for Grecian-style rooms sporting milk-white details. The Victorians favored deep, muted greens, often set off by crimson. Soft, dark "greenery yallery," as Gilbert and Sullivan dubbed it, and a brighter bottle green were two colors seen in flat, stylized Arts and Crafts wallpapers.

Right top: *Muted, moss green paint highlights the handsome, traditional woodwork in a sunny butler's pantry.*

Right bottom: *To emphasize the garden view, the windows wear graceful swags of rich green. Earthy red tones provide a classic foil.*

Clockwise (top left to right): *The unexpected juxtaposition of apple green and deep purple makes a bold statement in a contemporary bedroom. A forest shade becomes the background for country collectibles. Pale tints of pink and mint enhance in this spring-fresh living room. Hints of yellow, red, and blue make this green-on-green tableau work.*

Grayed greens, such as soft sage and moss, were long used in New England interiors and by Shaker craftsmen as subtle tints that look good by cool light. Bright yellow-greens—lime and pea soup—appeared in 1950s fabrics and tiles. Brighter still, they became fashion colors in the late 1960s, muting to deeper avocado tones in the earthier 1970s palette. Deep, clear greens, growing lighter in the 1990s, have been a staple of decorating in recent decades, possibly as a reflection of environmental interests or maybe just for their verdant serenity. Currently, acid or neon green is "the marker of the decade," according to Margaret Walch. "In fact, it might be *the* color of the decade." It is part of a trio of colors—acid green, yellow, and orange—that is being widely used in the 1990s.

purple: regal and highly individual

Purple was once the rarest and most prized of colors, reserved for royalty in ancient Rome, when twenty thousand murex shellfish were needed to produce dye enough for one yard of Tyrian purple cloth. True purple, equal amounts of red

Above: *In this dining room, purple walls with deep olive trim suggest a Victorian splendor, handsomely spared any excess clutter.*

Color palette: *Vivid hyacinth, vintage lavender, velvety purple, and flowery violet.*

design secret:
Untraditional wall
colors can make a
dramatic setting for
a collection of fine
antique furniture.

and blue, deepened with black, has had an up-and-down decorating career. One international fabric firm for years eschewed purple in its product offerings since the company's president considered it "vulgar." Some decorators feel that purple, used in quantity, has a yellowing afterimage that distorts other colors.

In the Victorian era, a soft purple, which the French dubbed "mauve" after the tender tint of mallow flowers, was the first aniline dye and a vogue color of the day. Purple resurfaced briefly in the iris-bright tints of Art Nouveau fabrics and glasswork. But then it was little seen until orchid turned up in the 1950s pastel palette, being especially favored in bathroom tile. It resurfaced once again, in darker, funkier form in the late 1960s. A light purple-toned pink was one of the 1980s Postmodern hues, used indoors and out. Though overlooked for a house's public spaces, purple in paler shades of lavender and violet has always held its decorative turf in bedrooms, where it's been appreciated for its fresh daintiness and the red component that makes it warm and flattering to skin tones.

Above: *An opulent carved and claw-footed settee, upholstered in crimson moiré fabric and gold cording, stands its own against the strong background hue. Dark baseboards intensify the deep, jewel-like colors.*

Above: *Eggplant shades of purple offer an intriguing sense of depth. In this kitchen, the dark richness is offset with plenty of white and natural light.*

Right: *Bouquets of lilacs enhance the delicate lavender color of the walls.*

Above: *Purple's whiff of unconventionality suits this comfortably futuristic living room, with its bold geometry and tactile surfaces. Complementary yellow, toned down to soft gold, warms the surroundings.*

Yet the paucity of purple in mainstream decorating has always made the choice seem particularly refreshing and fun, a bit theatrical and highly individual. Purple can be rich with personality. Like green, purple is a versatile merging of warm and cool, and by changing the proportions of the mix, you can tip the color into either camp. A purple with lots of red, ranging from light to dark violet-pink, burgundy, or magenta, can be lively and toasty-warm and as sweet as any pink. Strengthening its blue component creates intense violet shades or pale lavender, either with an emphasis on coolness. (See color palette on page 125.)

Because it's underpinned by such strong hues, a saturated purple is a vibrant, demanding color. Purples deepened with black, such as eggplant and plum, have an appealing sense of depth and mystery, especially on light-catching surfaces. Pastel versions of purple, either warm or cool according to their makeup, can be space-enhancing and romantic and look surprisingly formal dressed in white moldings and dark wood furniture.

Purple, with its dual nature, is affected by the company it keeps. It generally harmonizes with either of its constituent primaries, though it may join more smoothly with the color emphasized in its make-up. Contrasts will strengthen purple; a creamy tint, however, may be a more urbane foil than a strong yellow.

Lighting, too, will change the perception of purple: Yellowish illumination, as purple's complement, will mute the vibrancy, while standard cool fluorescents stress the blue. Sometimes a purple setting that seems cool by night can warm up surprisingly in the natural glow of day.

Above: *Soft lilac tints, gentle and flattering to skin tones, have long been favored for private nests. The pure white chaise and folding screen, plus a tender pink, hand-painted chest, add to this room's femininity.*

Left: *Colorful lobster buoys punctuate the ceiling of this children's room. The bold blue-purple and hot pink color scheme energizes the sloped planes of the ceiling and simple furnishings. Light reflected off the bright bedspreads adds a warm glow.*

essential
neutrals

though you won't find neutrals on the color wheel, it's hard to plan a scheme that doesn't incorporate at least some "no-color colors." Technically, the true neutrals are black, white, and gray, but for decorating, the category extends to off-whites and creams, beiges, and browns, as well as natural textures of wood, stone, rattan, and metals. Neutrals are the colors of nature or of simple "undecorated" materials, such as muslin, whitewash, leather, or clay. Yet without losing their relaxed, unfussy character, such hues can still underpin the most sophisticated settings. Easygoing, mixable neutrals and naturals often play a supporting role in a design, but given some imaginative direction, they're also capable of carrying the whole show.

Previous page: *The contrast of the all-white fabric against the wood tones emphasizes the curvy shape of French Provincial chaise.*

Below: *Gleaming wood, teamed with tactile rugs and upholstery in mellow tans and browns, is a nature-inspired color scheme that is influenced by the Arts and Crafts traditions.*

These understated choices have several selling points. They can flow unobtrusively to enhance a sense of space. The flow can even continue from room to room and support varied schemes along the way. In a room focused on a vivid, ever-expanding collection—teapots, rag dolls, or fine paintings—a low-key background enhances them all. If you crave a lipstick red armchair or turquoise silk curtains, some neutrals in the mix not only intensify the hues but also provide breathing space and visual relief to such vibrancy.

On a practical note, if expensive, harder-to-replace elements—the broadloom carpet, the bathroom fixtures—are kept fairly neutral, you can change walls or furniture on a whim. Darker neutrals tend to be forgiving of daily wear. But beyond their usefulness, neutrals can be charming and relaxing, a serene background to a hectic life. A room designed completely in neutrals, however, should exploit their subtleties without lapsing into monotony.

Even though they're short on color, neutrals offer their own kind of spectrum from light to dark and warm to cool. In a handful of variegated pebbles, you can observe nature's repertoire of grays, whites, and beiges. Beyond the tonal range from light to dark, neutrals often carry a tinge of color, which may be tricky to discern. If in doubt, hold swatches of primaries against a beige or gray and observe which hue it picks up.

When color takes a back seat, the spotlight is on texture and sheen. Beige can be gossamer silk, a nubby tweed, a stippled wall, or shimmering lacquer; gray can be dark charcoal, stone, or pastel oyster. Such shifts in tone and texture enliven an all-neutral scheme and determine whether it seems earthy or ethereal.

black and white: attractive opposites

In small-windowed Early American houses, fresh whitewash was a cheap, light-enhancing interior finish. White remains a decorating staple, whether for a nostalgic Victorian "cottage" parlor, a rugged Southwestern stuccoed room, or a minimalist Modern interior. Pure, bright white can be dazzling and make companion colors more luminous. A colorless backdrop emphasizes furniture and

Left: *Black is a bold decorating strategy in a powder room wrapped in dark laminates and tone-on-tone stripes. The elaborate mirror suits this dramatic setting.*

Color palette: *Glossy midnight black and linen white.*

artworks. It's also frequently invoked in kitchens and baths for an air of cleanliness and efficiency.

Pure white can be dainty as lace or boldly high tech, but it can also come across as cold and impersonal unless it's enriched with textures and accents. Also, warns designer Lyn Peterson, "White isn't always restful—your eye looks for some design or color it can hold onto." She adds, "White works in new, smooth interiors. Old bumpy walls might benefit from a bit of pattern." In a much-used environment, white is also going to demand attentive housekeeping to keep its purity.

Black adds drama and strong forms to a room, and until the twentieth century, it was generally used for accents. Touches of deep black define and deepen a room and render the accompanying colors darker and more jewel-like.

Left: *A black-and-white theme can link several graphic patterns. Against a low-key tan background, the upholstered bed joins a bold gingham check with more free-form designs; yellow accents provide a visual rest from the patterns.*

Below: *A crisp black-and-white floor, a design staple since the Renaissance, completes an entry decked in neoclassical wallpaper sharing the two-toned theme.*

Black has gradations from soft charcoal to darkest ebony, many with tints and undertones of red or blue. Texture determines the character of light-absorbing black: Matte textures make it denser, while glossy finishes seem livelier. Even with the bounce of reflective finishes, rooms heavy on black require brighter lighting.

Stark black and white, the ultimate contrast, can be a sophisticated minimalist treatment that highlights the shapes of furniture and architecture. (See color palette on page 133.) Though the combination seems up to the minute, it has precedents in old Dutch floors, turn-of-the-century tilework, and Art Deco ziggurats. A large-scale checkerboard floor is a perennial favorite—though in a high-traffic kitchen or foyer, it reveals dirt, both light and dark. Such a floor is easier to maintain if both surfaces are slightly mottled.

Such a sharp contrast naturally plays into geometric designs, which can be mixed freely if moderated by plain expanses. A pure black-and-white room tends to be a bit of a set-piece, since clutter diminishes the carefully wrought effect. It may suit short-stay rooms like hallways, perhaps with touches of black in adjoining rooms for unity. Almost any color

can join the pair, though bright, clear hues stand up best to their strong presence. The inherent warmth of wood, wicker, or sisal can also mellow the contrast.

cream: congenial and versatile

Cream is white touched with yellow for various tints of butter, parchment, or simply a hint of warmth. Cream shares white's characteristics, though it's never as stark. Since bright white paint wasn't available until after World War I (because titanium dioxide—a white pigment—wasn't discovered until the 1920s), creamy tones may better emulate the softer look of whitewash or now-banned lead-based paints in traditional or country rooms. Cream can seem rich and romantic, and the underlying

Left top: *Here, cream walls are a better choice than too-stark white because cream's warmth enhances the tones of the rich woods and the exotic leopard print.*

Left bottom: *White's purity lends a sense of clean serenity to this bedroom and emphasizes the room's geometry.*

Color palette: *Cream, breakwater white, petal white, and champagne.*

yellow lends a sunniness. Cream goes well with midtones and pumped-up pastels; sharp primaries may balance better with a clearer white, which makes a crisper, contrast.

White might seem like the simplest neutral—after all, the 1930s designer Elsie de Wolfe exhorted the aspiring decorator to have "plenty of optimism and white paint." Yet most whites in paint or fabric carry a whisper of another color, as anyone who's tried to match them will attest. Many whites are touched with the lightest pastel tints, though it may require the contrast of bright white moldings to make the color perceptible. Such tints can initiate the room's palette yet remain fairly accommodating. New York-based designer and paint authority Donald Kaufman gives depth to stark white by adding drops of various pure pigments to a white base, creating an almost subliminal effect as the changing light picks out different tints throughout the day. Just as in primaries, a white with a blue tone will seem cold, and a pink or yellow blush adds

Above: *Off-white with the barest hint of yellow plays up the ample natural light from the Palladian window and skylight. Pale pink provides subtle touches of rosy relief; the harlequin-patterned armoire adds a dose of another accent color—green.*

Left: *Soothing silver gray walls are invigorated by a canary yellow butterfly chair and tulips.*

Color palette: *Graphite, steel gray, mauve gray, and warm gray.*

a warmer glow. While perhaps not consciously noticeable, a very pale tint can unbalance a scheme or, more happily, can subtly reinforce the room's major color themes while remaining a neutral backdrop.

gray: soothing and sophisticated

Gray results from mixing black and white or blending complementary pairs. Its fine gradations run from almost-black graphite through warm dove shades to pastel oyster tints verging on white. Flat, clear gray tends to be dull and industrial, so many grays that appear in interiors are tinged with color. Gray

almost forms its own quieter color wheel: It can reflect a steel or stone blue cast or a greenish tone, or it may be warmed with a hint of pink or yellow. For more harmony, the gray should lightly echo the dominant color in the room.

Used as a contrast, gray tends to pick up its companion colors while toning down the overall impression. It mixes well with colors of equal depth, whether light or saturated. Less harsh than black, gray can still make a crisp line against white or

Far left: *Gray, freshened with white woodwork, fashions a sophisticated background for black-framed artworks and a pair of ebonized chairs.*

Left: *Weathered shades of gray and honey-colored wood in spare geometric forms creates a Zenlike serenity in a Japanese-influenced kitchen.*

cream or smooth out a black-and-white scheme without disrupting the achromatic quality.

browns: warm and comfortable

Brown, a blend of red and yellow, toned down with black, generally exudes homey comfort rather than high style. The brown family also encompasses wood's rainbow of tones, from ebony to yellow pine. Readily achieved with earth pigments and several dyes, brown has always been a decorating basic around the world. In the eighteenth century, woodwork was often painted and grained in dark reddish browns. In Victorian times, velvety brown took part in polychromatic schemes, teamed with yellows or purples. Subtle earthy tones shone in the leathers, woods, and copper of the Craftsman era.

Above: *Wood is a consummate mixer, ready to accompany other colors but a strong presence in its own right. In Arts and Crafts rooms, the rich range of wood tones creates a solid sort of beauty.*

Color palette: *Butterscotch, burnt sienna, chocolate, and beige.*

Deep browns need bright accents and plenty of light to keep coziness from crossing over to gloominess. Warm chocolate brown plays up the red component, while umber brown, which can approach black, is considerably cooler.

Tinting brown with white or gray introduces the whole array of beiges. Beige is often considered the ultimate neutral—a synonym for a non-

committal choice that goes with everything. And indeed it is a very useful, easygoing range. But beige can create a complex scheme all on its own, since it extends from creamy almost-white to rosy tints that approach peach, from sandy shades with a hint of blue or gray to beige with a sophisticated olive complexion.

Above: *The no-nonsense stainless steel cabinets seem more friendly when paired with the toasty beiges and browns of the tilework.*

Right: *The appeal of wood tones cuts across design boundries. Here, Prairie Style and Asian influences meet.*

Below: *An all-neutral scheme can range from pale to dark in a variety of textures. In this bedroom the gold-and-silver walls catch the light, while the matte textures of the chair and rug cozy up the setting.*

Color palette: *Putty, mushroom, cobblestone, and dark khaki.*

You need to discern these subtle undertones to use a beige effectively. A pinkish beige with red accents may be overwarm, where a sandy beige would be a cooling contrast.

ambiguous neutrals: complex and versatile

"A lot of the neutrals we're seeing are complex and wonderful," says designer and color consultant Rebecca Ewing. These "polychromatic" neutrals include hard-to-define full-bodied khakis, taupes, gray greens, or cooked-mushroom tints. (See color palette at left.) "You can't quite pin down the color, and over the course of the day it seems to change," she continues, "as the light brings out hints of gray or brown or purple."

With such rich neutrals, you may choose other elements as contrasts. Ambiguous neutrals team up well with rich, urbane hues. "It's easier to find a red shirt to go with khaki pants than to find another shade of khaki that looks good," notes designer Lyn Peterson. "The same holds true in a room. If you have a strong neutral, it's way easier to work with contrasts." These complex neutrals change as accompanying colors bring out differ-

design secret:
Layer color subtly
by using the same hue
in different values,
such as light, medium,
and dark beige, or a
variety of hues in one
value—for instance,
taupe, plum, and
forest green all in a
medium value.

ent aspects of their characters. A stone fireplace, for example, will appear more gray with a black leather couch or more light brown with a beige one. Also check how the shifts of light will influence these dense colors—an effect known as *metamerism*. Yet ambiguous neutrals still remain good mixers, with the versatility that makes neutrals so multifaceted.

Above: *Though the hazy grays and browns of this stonework could accompany any number of colors, the soft furnishings hew to the same deep neutral range.*

Right: *A midnight blue ottoman and throw add an unexpected dash of color to the sophisticated ambiguous gray walls and white wainscot.*

create style with painted techniques

decorative painting techniques transform paint, the standard quick cover-up, into a one-of-a-kind finish. Like wallcoverings, they can lend a plain expanse a sense of dimension, texture, and pattern with an interplay of hues. But decorative painting offers added flexibility: It allows you to control both color and pattern and to embellish floors and furniture as well as walls. Instead of spending hours, for example, pursuing a wallpaper pattern to work with *both* the pink tile and the tan bathtub, you might instead use the time to layer on a subtle painted finish to solve the decorating problem. While certain painted effects require fine artistic skills, many require only patience, practice, and preparation to achieve satisfyingly dramatic results.

Until the late-nineteenth-century advent of premixed paints, house painting was the province of the master craftsman, who in a long apprenticeship learned the art of mixing pigments on-site and applying decorative paint finishes. Journeyman painters traveled throughout Early America, ready to mahogany-grain a pine doorway, ring a room in stencils, or marble a fireplace. This chapter reviews those decorative painting techniques so that you can create them at home.

before you begin

Don't skimp on preparation. Though some painted finishes help disguise less-than-perfect walls, take time to scrape, patch, and sand any cracks, holes, or peeling areas, and to wash greasy walls or woodwork. (If damaged paint dates to pre-1980, it may contain lead, which is a health hazard. Have it tested, and hire a specialist to scrape and sand the lead-based paint.)

Paint Basics

Whether your painting ambitions are plain or fancy, a paint store with a knowledgeable staff can help

Previous page: *A red-and-black checkerboard pattern is a historically appropriate painted effect for this Early American staircase.*

Above: *Influenced by Monet's paintings, hazy, impressionistic wall murals in soft pastels contribute to this restful bedroom's Old World opulence.*

you zero in on the right products and techniques. Buy quality paints and tools, such as artists' brushes and rollers, which more than pay back a nominal cost difference in easier application and better coverage.

Most interior paints are either alkyd-resin paints (oil-based) or latex varieties (water-based). Oil and water don't mix, and generally neither do the paints based on them. For multilayered effects, stick to one type or the other.

Alkyd paints are somewhat more lustrous, translucent, and harder-wearing. But some alkyds, and the solvents needed for cleaning up, are toxic and combustible, requiring good work-site ventilation and special disposal methods.

Professional decorative painters often prefer slower-drying alkyds, which allow more time to achieve complex special effects. Alkyd paints are better suited to techniques such as combing and rag rolling, where glaze is brushed on in sections and then manipulated.

Latex paints, which now approach alkyd's durability and textural range, are nontoxic and quick-drying, and they clean up with soap and water.

design secret:

To add depth to wall colors, use a white base coat under a tinted glaze. Light will reflect off the white, making the glaze seem translucent.

Below: *Delicately soft-edged murals, which require advanced techniques to create, become a fitting background to the room's classically elegant antiques.*

Right top: *Stencils can be a subtle treatment when the colors are kept subdued and closely allied to the background tint.*

Right bottom: *Decorative painting can enliven small spaces. Here, an exuberant bathroom mural draws inspiration from cartoons.*

Most amateurs find latex paint easier to deal with and capable of creating many popular decorative finishes.

In general, latex paints are best suited to effects that are dabbed on over the base coat, as in sponging or stenciling. The short drying time can even be an advantage, since the job goes faster and mistakes can be expeditiously painted over and redone.

painted effects

While certain painted finishes demand artistic skills, many are within reach of a beginner working with care and detailed instructions. Practice the techniques, and try out color combinations on a primed piece of hardboard— even professional decorative painters often do a trial run. Let the sample dry before rendering judgment, by both natural and artificial light. (A blow-dryer will speed the drying process.)

An old furniture piece or a large wastebasket may be less intimidating than a big, blank wall for an initial foray into decorative painting. Also, many large painting projects run more smoothly with a team: One person lays on glaze and blends the edges, while the other keeps on texturing.

Glazing Techniques

One big, loose family of decorative painted finishes encompasses "broken color" effects. These effects begin with a fully dried, painted base coat,

Above: A seascape mural of sunbathers and windsurfers gives this child's room a sense of adventure and individuality. Note how the mural was designed around existing furnishings such as the bookshelf.

which peeks through the upper layer of textured glaze. A *glaze* is a translucent coating with a small amount of pigment suspended in a clear medium. Glazes can be bought ready to be tinted with artists' oils or acrylics; or they can be mixed on-site by thinning latex paint with water or alkyds with solvents.

Broken-color techniques are an easy way to create an inviting atmosphere. A base coat and glaze in closely related colors, such as a warm beige and fawn, form a soft, understated texture. A stronger contrast, such as cream and bleached

Below: *Sponging can fashion a soft, cloudlike impression, particularly effective in subtle, low-contrast color combinations. The mottled pink walls blend well with the antique oak furniture and cast-iron bed.*

terra cotta, creates a bolder pattern and requires greater precision in the coverage. Here are a few popular broken-color painting approaches:

Sponging is a fairly quick and easy favorite for beginners, capable of looking either crisply patterned or soft and blurry. (It can also be an interesting remedy for a paint job that turned out a bit too dark or too light.) A damp natural sponge is lightly dipped in glaze, blotted, and dabbed on the wall with a light, random touch. Keep the prints clear, and rinse and wring the sponge occasionally. Different colors can be layered on as each application dries, though the effect is best kept subtle.

Ragging is similar to sponging, with crumpled, lint-free rags used to dab on the paint in a bold pattern. In rag rolling, the glaze is brushed on, then partly removed and textured by rolling the still-wet surface with a "sausage" of rags or, for a rough texture, crumpled paper or plastic wrap. For consistent results, practice the technique beforehand and have a ready supply of rags.

Stippling also selectively removes the wet glaze by jabbing it with brush bristles to reveal the base coat in a hazy speckle. You can use a variety of stippling brushes; softer bristles give a

Above: *Skillful painting with layered, translucent stains transforms a standard wood floor into a faux parquet. The trick is to lay out the design to scale on grid paper before you attempt the pattern on the floor.*

more mottled finish. Practice maintaining consistent pressure on each pass. Stippling is a soft effect, even with strong color contrasts.

Sometimes the term stippling refers to an opposite technique, where glaze is applied with a pouncing motion using a wide, stiff brush.

Dragging, also called *strié*, grains the wet, brushed-on glaze with long, smooth top-to-bottom strokes of a special long-haired brush. The long stroke takes a steady hand and an even surface to produce an elegant, silken look.

Combing resembles dragging but with bolder stripes laid down by a variety of steel, rubber, or metal combs, or a squeegee with irregular teeth notched into it. The wet, thick glaze can be combed in waves, zigzags, overlapped semicircles, or checkerboards. Bolder patterns generally have a lively folksy effect and may look best confined to a small area—a bathroom floor or a wainscot or a furniture piece, such as a trunk or sideboard.

Color washing is a mellow, weathered effect achieved with diluted glazes, which are brushed on in random, overlapped

design secret:
For broken color techniques, don't apply the glaze too thickly. It will form a slow-drying skin that is unmanageable.

crosshatching and softened while wet with a sponge, rag, or dry brush. Multiple coats in varied colors lend a sense of depth and hide imperfections.

Spattering tends to be lively and offbeat, with random sprays of dots flicked across a surface using a brush or a long bundle of twigs dipped in glaze. Spattering is easier on a horizontal plane, such as a floor, but even then it takes practice to control the pattern.

Great Pretenders

Another family of decorative paint techniques are faux finishes:

Wood graining may incline toward fantasy or realism. This more specialized technique generally involves dragging with specific graining brushes and detailing with "rockers"—rubber combs to layer on the distinctive grains, knots, and whorls

Above: *America's design heritage includes a trove of folk painted finishes. Here, a grained trunk and folk-art-painted chest deepen the flavor of a traditional room. The trunk was combed in fanlike, overlapping half circles.*

Left (top to bottom): *At first glance, this stately garnet red dining room appears to center on a classic Queen Anne dining set. But a closer examination reveals that a space-saving banquette bench has been humorously portrayed as a line-up of trompe l'oeil chairs.*

of such exotic woods as bird's-eye maple, burled oak, and mahogany.

Trompe l'oeil compositions are the most theatrical faux effects because they "fool the eye" with seemingly three-dimensional scenes: a vista-filled window, birds perched on the chair rail, or gloves on an entry table. True *trompe l'oeil* demands an artist's skill. Lacking that, a homeowner may enjoy creating simple flat murals or copying a picture from a book or postcard to a wall. To transfer a picture, enlarge it as necessary with a photocopying

Below: *A combination of techniques turns a plain mantel and built-in cabinetry into eye-catching elements. The mantel is faux painted to look like rose marble, an advanced but achievable technique. The flower bouquets adorning the cabinet doors and mantel panels were stenciled, then detailed by hand.*

machine. Draw a grid over it, and sketch a scaled-up version of the grid lightly on the wall. Then copy the picture, square by square.

Faux stone techniques generally focus on the myriad varieties of marble. Faux-marbling involves many different techniques, all requiring practice and close study of the real stone. The effect usually starts with darker and lighter colorwashed streaks of glaze, softened and distressed with brushes, sponges, and rags. Fine brushes or feathers apply the veining, delicate and bold. Skilled decorative painters also evoke other stones, such as the fine-grained spatter of a multi-colored granite or vivid lapis or malachite for small decorative touches.

Pretty as Pictures

Stenciling is a more accessible pictorial painted effect, a craft with a long folk history. Stenciling can be a quick dash of a simple country motif or a delicately shaded multicolor composition.

design secret:
When applying a decorative finish on a wall, work in small sections and always stop at a corner to prevent visible lines.

Clockwise (left to right): *Because stenciling has a long folk tradition, the classic motifs instantly evoke a sense of the past. In the breezy geometry of its painted-on chair rail, a featureless wall gains urbane personality. Printed fabrics can inspire stencil patterns—or you can find more offbeat sources such as these stencils from gravestone rubbings.*

In addition to the wide menu of precut stencils available, you can make your own from heavy acetate or cardboard that has been waterproofed and reinforced by a spray-on acrylic. You can find inspiration for stencil motifs in books on architectural ornaments as well as fabrics, wallpaper, and pottery. Adapt the pattern by simplifying it to a bold outline.

Thick stenciling paint is applied in light, pouncing dabs with a small sponge or a well-blotted short-bristled brush. For a shading effect, start from the bottom of the stencil and work upward.

Block printing is another way of scattering on simple, graphic motifs. Printing blocks, such as stamps, can be bought or created by cutting designs into sponges, potatoes, or other firm materials, or by attaching a small object to a blank printing block. While a certain irregularity is part of the charm, block prints can be lightly touched-up with a fine brush.

Block printing makes quick work of decorating small objects, such as containers, chair backs, and picture frames. When working on larger surfaces, such as walls or tabletops, decide before you start whether the pattern will be applied randomly or at measured intervals.

Above: *"Broken color" finishes suggest a soft-edged, time-worn surface, especially when the colors work together harmoniously. Here, light green and yellow glazes cover a white base coat.*

the
future
of color

in your design imagination, your color schemes know no bounds. But once you set out in the world to collect samples and buy the ingredients, you might find other forces at work. Are you going to find the products and patterns that you picture in your mind's eye? And how do manufacturers, who have an endless range of possibilities to choose from, decide which colors they're going to bet their profits on? In the realities of the marketplace, you may find that a favorite color is hard to locate, as if banished. Or you're intrigued by unexpected hues and combinations that—also as if by decree—seem to appear everywhere. Maybe it's a color you remember from your grandmother's parlor or from your cluttered dorm room. What's going on here?

Previous page: *The colors in this living room are not haphazardly chosen. Forecasters try to anticipate whether jewel-like shades of sapphire blue and emerald green or a desert hue like terra cotta are the next "new" colors.*

Right: *An unconventional juxtaposition of colors—violet, soft lemon, and pale lime—plays up this room's futuristic flair. But will consumers buy these novel hues?*

Manufacturers, whether they're making toothbrushes or sweaters, sheets or lamps, know that color makes the sale. A business can't make choices by personal preferences or airy notions of beauty—to a manufacturer, a beautiful color is one that sells. To anticipate the desires of fickle customers, manufacturers and product designers lean on the color-forecasting industry.

the color cartel?

That color-forecasting industry includes dozens of organizations and individuals who seek to predict hues that will fly off the shelves at a point sixteen to twenty-one months in the future. The oldest, the Color Association of the United States (CAUS), was founded in 1917 by American textile companies stranded by World War I without Europe's dyes and fashion directions. The Color Council, a relative latecomer, has become a force in home furnishings. The Color Marketing Group (CMG), a nonprofit

design secret:
Let nature—in the form of, say seashells, flowers, and rocks— inspire your color combinations. Then find materials similar to those hues and textures.

organization, emerged to sort out the color chaos of the early 1960s; today its 1,500-plus members meet in industry-focused panels to seek consensus on such questions as "Where is yellow going?"

Forecasters generally supply clients with "color cards" indicating current, relatively stable favorites and more daring fashion-forward choices. They also suggest the palette's overall thrust—more muted and dark, more clear and mid-toned. "Color's general direction is important because any one color can be used to different effects," says CMG president Melanie Wood. "A particular yellow paired with red and orange might seem very warm, but with white and blue, it would turn fresh and crisp. Which of those moods is the customer looking for?" A general palette is also translated differently by different industries; major investments like flooring naturally tend toward more conservative shades than ephemeral tabletop items.

Colors run in cycles, as we embrace a novel hue, grow accustomed to it, and eventually drop it in search of new sensations. What's old does become new again; the 1980s and 1990s periodically recycled colors from the previous decades. Traditionally, a "new" color first appears in the volatile clothing industry, with a few trickling down to the slower-paced

Above: *Current color trends foster an individualized approach to design. This medley of strong hues—pink, yellow, purple, and blue—summons up a lively tropical atmosphere in a simply furnished seaside setting.*

home furnishings market. But today's fashionable colors circulate faster, often buzzing through both sectors almost simultaneously.

And what drives these cycles? Color forecasters look first to the economy: Good times tend to promote upbeat colors, prompting impulse purchases, while leaner times tend toward more practical, subdued choices. Certain social movements may be reflected in the palette; the 1970s focus on "natural" prompted an earthy palette, while environmental concerns fostered a wealth of greens in the late 1980s and 1990s. Blockbuster museum exhibits, political events that spotlight

Above: *Easy eclecticism and lush textures are strong current trends. Cheerful colors—sunny yellow, cobalt blue, and lime green—and woven surfaces meet harmoniously in this comfortable living room.*

particular countries, pacesetting public figures, and popular movies all contribute to an era's "look."

Color forecasters cast a wide net for influences, keeping tabs on current and upcoming events, high-profile stores and restaurants, the media, and fashion and home-furnishing trade shows, domestically and abroad. A certain amount of consensus usually emerges between different forecasting organizations. "We're all here in the present together," notes CAUS's director, Margaret Walch, "and the forecast is based on the present and the immediate past." Forecasters get a feel for how color tastes change: If green is strong, it won't just vanish. Rather it might merge into a range of neutrals like sage and celadon or "bridge" into green-yellows or green-blues, which in turn might grow clearer. The toughest trick is to logically extend the current range with colors new enough to be appealing and compelling, yet not completely without precedent.

Forecasting remains more an art than science, requiring a certain amount of instinct and sensitivity to hard-to-define factors. Color forecasters try to tune into the public's mood and driving concerns. Is it an up-tempo, economically stable time, when consumer tastes may lean toward the adventurous? Or are people feeling cautious and inclined to stick to tried-and-true favorites?

Above: *A soft tint of pink—a "bridge" color for red—toned into a warm neutral is a classic choice for this relaxing room.*

Above: *Spicy tints of saffron and paprika in this living room reflect Eastern influences that are broadening and brightening current color palettes. The bamboo table and chair add texture and play against the shiny pillow fabric.*

Right: *Green, a popular choice in recent decades, has diversified into a broader range. Here, a deep olive, freshened with pure white, lends a formal richness. Gilded stars and lighting fixtures, as well as the mirrored fireplace surround, add shine to a room of matte surfaces.*

Even then, the industry is occasionally blindsided by unexpected developments.

time to reflect

Many forecasters feel that America's mainstream home furnishing colors are changing more slowly than before. "We're in an evolutionary palette," says Walch. "There's so much coming at people, they're seeking comfort in the familiar."

Catherine Stein, president of The Color Council, agrees that trends are slowing down and that the public is less interested in flipping quickly through fads. But she also notes that generalities about color are elusive in such a wide, splintered market. "America is not a melting pot—it's a salad bar," she points out. In the 1960s, she explains, everyone wanted avocado green rugs and harvest gold appliances, but today's manufacturers have to pursue niche markets of various ethnic and demographic groups. "It used to be, a company was a success with the top three towel colors, but now it needs nine," she continues. "Consumers are used to a tremendous range of choices, and you can't take that away from them. Today's colors represent a celebration of the individual."

Thus current color trends turn not so much on progression as proliferation: "We see different palettes running concurrently," observes CMG's Melanie Wood. "Soft pastels are there right alongside punchy brights. You can't say 'out' and 'in' so neatly anymore."

Some of the influences in the mix: an Asian contribution of "embroidery" brights in dense patterns; a Mediterranean and Middle Eastern array of spicy yellow-golds and rich reds; and a youthful, urban palette of citrusy yellows, greens, and oranges—reflecting an audience easy with the "hypercolors" of the TV and computer screen. But the next color-saturated generation, in the demands of fashion, jokes Stein, may well "rebel to beige."

Technology is also diversifying color with dramatic surface treatments. Pearlescent or iridescent finishes, layered or flecked effects, faux suede or stone textures all give depth and complexity to subtle hues.

design secret:
Create a room-by-room progression of colors from light to dark. For example, a peach hallway can lead into a terra cotta dining room, followed by a pumpkin kitchen.

Color forecasters admit that to some extent their prophecies can be self-fulfilling. If tastemakers predict and manufacturers listen, certain colors will appear in the stores. But they may well stay there if they prove to be a miscalculation. "We can't dictate. We can only interpret what we see happening and translate that into salable colors," says CMG's Wood. "You can't force a color on the public. The consumer can always get even by refusing to buy it!"

"Forecasters exist to bring some coordination to the market, which works to a homeowner's benefit," says CAUS's Walch. In addition to some compatibility across the board, specific industries can share palettes, allowing, for instance, matching nonskid tile and ceramic bathroom fixtures. "But from the consumer's point of view," she concedes, "there are going to be certain colors that are hard to find."

What are some options when you love a color that's fallen from grace? It might just take more diligent shopping. The pursuit of niche markets means that almost every color is out there somewhere. Antique

Above: *Crisp white on the moldings and the chair slipcovers keeps the fashionable taupe color scheme in this dining room light and airy rather than drab.*

Opposite (clockwise): *Fashions come and go, but colors tend to maintain their emotional connections. The sunny glow of soft yellow is a perfect wake-up for a morning person's bedroom. The younger generation, raised on hyper-colors possible in current technology, may drive the home-furnishings palette toward a still broader spectrum of choices. Soothing neutrals, long tied to traditional interiors, are a decorating mainstay.*

Clockwise (left to right): *Color forecasters try to predict the public's taste when choosing a hue. Consumers may be receptive to unexpected color combinations, such as yellow-green walls and a pale blue sofa. On the other hand, stoplight yellow paired with robin's egg blue and cherry red may be more to their liking. Or are they in the mood for yellow walls that have been softened to a flaxen color?*

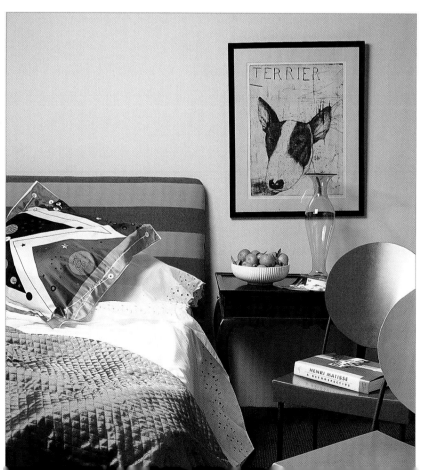

and secondhand stores are also sources of vintage colors. Retailers or to-the-trade sources specializing in imported products may offer some offbeat color directions that are popular in Europe.

the last word: obtaining your color

If home-furnishing fabrics aren't yielding up the right color choice, you might look across the aisle at the dressmaking textiles, where you can find different looks, suitable for lighter-duty applications. And you can always incorporate your chosen color with paint, since custom colors are easy to get. And you can hang on for the next turn of the color cycle.

Being open to color trends can be fun, as a way to consider a fresh possibility or add an up-to-the-minute accessory. Noticing a lot of housewares in yellow, for instance, might suggest that a few sunny touches are just what your kitchen needs. "But don't follow trends for their own sake," advises The Color Council's Stein. "Who wants to live with someone else's idea of a hip color?" Wildly trendy colors also tend to date a room rather quickly.

The dictates of fashion should not be the overriding force in your home. Pulling together a scheme that makes you and your family feel good, that wears well day to day, and that shines with a bit of your own personality counts as a decorating success story.

GLOSSARY

Accent: In a room scheme, a small area of intense color that contrasts, either in hue or tone, with the lighter or more muted prevailing colors. Often provided by accessories and trimmings, accents add detail and draw the eye to various elements.

Achromatic: Lacking color—black, gray, or white.

Advancing Colors: Warm, saturated colors that seem to come forward toward the viewer. Advancing colors can make rooms seem more cozy and objects slightly larger.

Analogous Scheme: see Harmonious Color Scheme.

Color Wheel: A pie-shaped diagram showing the range and relationships of pigment and dye colors. Three equidistant wedge-shaped slices are the primaries; in between are the secondary and tertiary colors into which the primaries combine. Though represented as discrete slices, the hues form a continuum.

Complementary Colors: Hues directly opposite each other on the color wheel. As the strongest contrasts, complements tend to intensify each other. A color can be grayed by mixing it with its complement.

Contrasting Color Scheme: A combination involving choices from opposite sides of the color wheel. Strong contrasts create dynamic schemes, though muted or tinted versions are more harmonious.

Cool Colors: A loose division of the color wheel that includes the range of blues, greens, blue-greens, and blue-violets. Cool colors, particularly when pale, tend to be retreating colors.

Harmonious Color Scheme: Also called analogous, a combination focused on neighboring hues on the color wheel. The shared underlying color generally gives such schemes a coherent flow.

Hue: Another term for specific points on the pure, clear range of the color wheel.

Intensity: See Saturation.

Neutrals: Technically, pure white, black, and gray. In decorating, the term extends to grays and blacks with subtle tinges of color and off-whites, as well as a range of natural creams, beiges, and browns.

Primary Colors: Red, blue, or yellow, which, in pigments, can't be produced by mixing other colors. Primaries plus black and white, in turn, combine to make all the other hues.

Retreating Colors: Generally cool, pale hues that seem to recede from the viewer. Retreating colors can foster spatial illusions and make objects less obtrusive.

Saturation: The strength or purity of a color, determined by the amount and clarity of pigment.

Secondary Colors: A mix of two primaries. The secondaries are orange, green, and purple.

Shade: A color darkened with the addition of black or the color's complement. Maroon is a shade of red.

Tertiary Colors: A mix of a primary and secondary that produces a range of complex colors, such as blue-green, yellow-green, and red-orange.

Tint: A color lightened with white toward a pastel range. Pink is a tint of red.

Tone: A grayed version of a color—that is, terra cotta is a tone of orange. More loosely, tone refers to a color's density and light reflectance, as determined by the proportions of pigment, white, and black in its composition. Colors of similar tone—a group of pastels or of dark, muted shades—tend to be harmonious. An overall room scheme, however, generally benefits from some tonal variations.

Value: The lightness or darkness of a color, running from a low-value shade to a high-value pastel tint. Value varies with the amount of white or black in the color's composition.

Warm Colors: On a color wheel, the range of reds, yellows, oranges and red-purples. Warm colors, especially when saturated, tend to advance.

CREDITS

page 1: *Photographer:* Francis Hammond. page 2: *Photographer:* Rob Gray. page 6: *Photographer:* Alan Shortall; *Designer:* Todd Schwebel. page 8: *Photographer (left):* Mark E. Gibson. *Photographer (right):* Mark Lohman; *Designer:* Janet B. Lohman. page 9: *Photographer (left):* Sam Gray; *Designer:* Bierly-Drake Assoc. *Photographer (right):* David Phelps, courtesy of *American Homestyle.* page 10: *Photographer (right):* Steve Gross and Susan Daley. *Photographer (right):* Mark Lohman; *Designer:* Janet B. Lohman. page 11: *Photographer (right):* Jessie Walker; *Designer:* Diane Wendall. *Photographer (right):* Lilo Raymond. page 12: *Photographer:* Brian Vanden Brink. page 14: *Photographer:* Steven Mays; *Designer:* Richard Smith. page 15: *Photographer:* Brian Vanden Brink; *Architects:* Centerbrook Architects. page 16: *Photographer (top):* Mike Moreland. *Photographer (bottom):* Brian Vanden Brink. page 17: *Photographer:* Steven Mays; *Designer:* Richard Smith. page 18: *Photographer:* Doug Keister; *Painter:* Esther Canalepich. page 19: *Photographer (top):* Mark Lohman; *Designer:* Janet B. Lohman. *Photographer (bottom):* Brian Vanden Brink. page 20: *Photographer:* Rob Gray. page 21: *Photographer:* Jessie Walker. page 22-23: *Photographer:* David Phelps, courtesy of *American Homestyle; Designer:* Max King. page 23: *Photographer:* Randy Wells/Tony Stone Images. page 24: *Photographer:* Grey Crawford/Beate Works; *Designer:* Lori Erenberg. page 25: *Photographer:* Gordon Beall; *Designer:* Sroka Design. page 26: *Photographers:* Steven Gross & Susan Daley. page 27: *Photographer:* Tria Giovan. page 28: *Photographer:* Steven Mays; *Designer:* John Fortney. page 29: *Photographer:* Steve Gross and Susan Daley. page 30: *Photographer (left):* Francis Hammond. *Photographer (right):* Mark Lohman; *Designer:* Janet B. Lohman. page 31: *Photographer:* Stephen Cridland; *Architect:* John Hasenberg. page 32: *Photographer:* Brian Vanden Brink; *Designer:* Drysdale Assoc. page 33: *Photographer (left):* Brian Vanden Brink; *Architect:* Stephen Blatt Architects. *Photographer (right):* Rob Melnychuk; *Designers:* Jim Brown and Matt Vanderwerff. page 34: *Photographer:* Kari Haavisto; *Architect:* Anne McCutcheon Lewis. page 36: *Photographer (top):* Sam Gray; *Designer:* Bierly-Drake Assoc. *Photographer (bottom):* Mark Lohman; *Designer:* Janet B. Lohman. page 39: *Photographer:* Mark Lohman; *Designer:* Janet B. Lohman. page 40: *Photographer:* Jack Parsons. page 41: *Photographer:* Mike Moreland. page 42: *Photographer:* Brian Vanden Brink; *Designer:* Jane Langmuir. page 44: *Photographer:* Steven Mays; *Designer:* Richard Smith. page 45: *Photographer:* David Phelps; *Architect:* James O'Connor. page 46: *Photographer:* David Phelps, courtesy of *American Homestyle.* page 47: *Photographer:* Anne Gummerson; *Designer:* Arnot & McComas. page 48: *Photographer (top):* Lilo Raymond. *Photographer (bottom):* David Phelps; *Architect:* James O'Connor. page 49: *Photographer:* Steve Gross and Susan Daley. page 50: *Photographer:* Jack Parsons. page 51: *Photographer:* Mark Lohman; *Designer:* Janet B. Lohman. page 52: *Photographer:* Mark Lohman; *Designer:* Janet B. Lohman. page 53: *Photographer:* Rob Melnychuk; *Designer:* Josette Whist. page 54: *Photographer:* Steve Gross & Susan Daley. page 56: *Photographer:* Brian Vanden Brink; *Architect:* Centerbrook Architects. page 57: *Photographer (left & right):* Robert Perron; *Architect:* P. V. Svigals. Architects. page 58: *Photographer:* Mark Samu; *Architects:* Sears & Sears. page 59: *Photographer:* Mark Lohman; *Designer:* Janet B. Lohman. page 60: *Photographer (top):* Hal Lott. *Photographer (bottom):* Francis Hammond; *Designer:* piadesign. page 61: *Photographer:* Sam Gray; *Designer:* Bierly-Drake Assoc. page 62: *Photographer:* Jessie Walker; *Designer:* Diane Wendall. page 63: *Photographer:* Phillip Ennis; *Designer:* Michael DeSantis. page 64: *Photographer:* Brian Vanden Brink; *Architect:* John Gillespie.

page 64-65: *Photographer:* Brian Vanden Brink; *Designer:* Drysdale Assoc. page 66: *Photographer:* Holly Stickley; *Designer:* George Tsaconas. page 68: *Photographer (left):* Mark Samu; *Designer:* Eileen Boyd Design. page 69: *Photographer (top):* Mark Lohman; *Designer:* Janet B. Lohman. *Photographer (bottom):* Frances Hammond. page 70-71: *Photographer (clockwise):* Frances Hammond. *Photographer:* Rob Melnychuk; *Painted Furniture Artist:* Rita Monaco. *Photographers:* Steve Gross & Susan Daley. page 73: *Photographer:* Rob Melnychuk. page 74: *Photographer:* Tom Yee. page 76: *Photographer:* Steve Gross & Susan Daley. page 78: *Photographer:* Melabee M Miller; *Fabric:* Waverly (#647020 Ottoman in Royal). page 80: *Photographer (clockwise):* Eric Roth; *Designer:* Veronique Louvet. *Photographer:* Eric Roth. *Photographer:* Brian Vanden Brink; *Architect:* Stephen Foote. page 82: *Photographer:* Mark Samu; *Architects:* Sears & Sears. page 84: *Photographers:* Steve Gross and Susan Daley. page 86: *Photographer:* Mark Samu; *Architects:* Sears & Sears. page 87: *Photographer:* Michael Moreland. page 88-89: *Photographer (top):* Hal Lott. *Photographer:* Rob Melnychuk; *Designer:* Vignette Design. *Photographer:* David Phelps, courtesy of *Woman's Day; Designer:* Charles Riley. page 90: *Photographer:* AR3; *Designers:* Wiseman & Gale. page 91: *Photographer (top):* Nancy Hill; *Designer:* Anne Mullin Interiors. *Photographer (bottom):* Sam Gray; *Designer:* Bierly-Drake Assoc. page 92: *Photographer:* Paul Schumm. page 93: *Photographer:* Mark Samu; *Designer:* Sears & Sears. page 94: *Photographer:* Al Teufen; *Designer:* Interiorworks. page 95: *Photographer:* Francis Hammond; *Designer:* piadesign. page 96: *Photographer:* Jessie Walker; *Designer:* Diane Wendall. page 97: *Photographer:* Stephen Cridland; *Designer:* Miller/Hull. page 98: *Photographer:* Mark Lohman; *Designer:* Janet B. Lohman. page 99: *Photographer:* Mark Lohman; *Designer:* Janet B. Lohman. page 100: *Photographer:* Steven Mays; *Designer:* John Fortney. page 101: *Photographer:* Bruce McCandless. page 102: *Photographer:* David Phelps, courtesy of *Woman's Day; Designer:* Charles Riley. page 104: *Photographer:* Rob Melnychuk; *Designer:* Dennis Garritty, Preston's Interiors. page 105: *Photographer:* Mark Lohman; *Designer:* Janet B. Lohman. *Photographer (clockwise):* Mark Lohman; *Designer:* Janet B. Lohman. *Photographers:* Steve Gross and Susan Daley. *Photographer:* Bruce McCandless. *Photographer:* Lilo Raymond. page 107: *Photographer:* Rob Melnychuk; *Designer:* Dennis Garritty, Preston's Interiors. page 108-109: *Photographer (clockwise):* Nancy Hill; *Designer:* Ann Mullin: Interiors. *Photographer:* Jessie Walker; *Designer:* Blair Baby. *Photographer:* Mark Lohman; *Designer:* Janet B. Lohman. page 110: *Photographer:* Mark Samu; *Designer:* Sears & Sears. page 111: *Photographer:* Nancy Hill; *Designer:* Deborah T. Lipner. page 112: *Photographer (left):* Steven Mays; *Designer:* John Fortney. *Photographer (right):* Rob Melnychuk; *Artist:* Rita Monaco. page 113: *Photographer:* Steve Gross and Susan Daley. page 114: *Photographer (top):* Lilo Raymond. *Photographer (bottom):* Rob Melnychuk; *Designer:* Wendy Williams Watt. page 115: *Photographer:* Lilo Raymond. page 116: *Photographer:* Steve Gross and Susan Daley. page 118: *Photographer:* Brian Vanden Brink; *Architect:* Rob Whitten. page 119: *Photographer (top):* Steve Gross and Susan Daley. *Photographer (bottom):* Brian Vanden Brink; *Designer:* Margaret Morfit. page 120-21: *Photographer (clockwise):* Melabee M Miller; *Designer:* Tracey Stephens. *Photographer:* Eric Roth; *Designer:* Christine Lane, CLC Interior Design. *Photographer:* Brian Vanden Brink; *Location:* Farnsworth Art Museum. page 122: *Photographer:* Sam Gray; *Designer:* Bierly-Drake Assoc. page 123: *Photographer (top):* Brian Vanden Brink. *Photographer (bottom):*

Michael Moreland. **page 124:** *Photographer (clockwise):* Rob Melnychuk; *Designer:* Kelly Sanderson. *Photographer:* Rob Melnychuk; *Designer:* Peryle Magnuson. *Photographer:* Nancy Hill; *Designer:* Karyne Johnson, Panache Interior. *Photographer:* Jack Parsons. **page 125:** *Photographer:* Alan Shortall; *Designer:* Todd Schwebel. **page 126:** *Photographer:* Alan Shortall; *Designer:* Todd Schwebel. **page 127:** *Photographer (top):* Rob Melnychuk; *Designer:* Wendy Williams Watt. *Photographer (bottom):* Lilo Raymond. **page 128:** *Photographer:* Rob Melnychuk; *Designer:* Kelly Sanderson. **page 129:** *Photographer (top):* Al Teufen; *Designer:* Interiorworks. *Photographer (bottom):* Brian Vanden Brink. **page 130:** *Photographer:* Lilo Raymond, courtesy of *Linens and Lace* by Trish Foley (Clarkson Potter). **page 132:** *Photographer:* Rob Gray. **page 133:** *Photographer:* Rob Melnychuk; *Designer:* Dennis Garritty, Preston's. **page 134:** *Photographer:* Brian Vanden Brink; *Designer:* Drysdale Assoc. **page 135:** *Photographer:* Brian Vanden Brink. **page 136:** *Photographer:* Rob Melnychuk; *Designer:* Wendy Williams Watt. *Photographer:* Lilo Raymond. **page 137:** *Photographer:* George Mattei; *Designer:* Acorn Design. **page 138-139:** *Photographer (clockwise):* Lilo Raymond. *Photographer:* Stephen Cridland. *Photographer:* Eric Roth; *Architect:* Robert Miklos, Schwartz: Silver Architects. **page 140:** *Photographer:* Rob Melnychuk; *Designer:* Bernstein & Gold. **page 141:** *Photographer (top):* Phillip Ennis; *Designer:* Gail Greene. *Photographer (bottom):* Jessie Walker. *Designers:* Kay McCarthy and Alfie McAdams. **page 142:** *Photographer:* Woody Cady; *Designer:* Ron Becker. **page 143:** *Photographer (top):* Phillip Ennis; *Designer:* Gail Whiting. *Photographer (bottom):* Rob Melnychuk; *Designer:* Wendy Williams Watt. **page144:** *Photographer:* Brian Vanden Brink. **page 146:** *Photographer:* Mark Samu; *Designer:* Mayo De Lucci. **page 147:** *Photographer:* Mark Samu; *Designer:*

Mayo De Lucci. **page 148:** *Photographer (top):* Steve Gross and Susan Daley. *Photographer (bottom):* Rob Melnychuk; *Mural Artist:* Rita Monaco. **page 149:** *Photographer:* Mark Lohman; *Designer:* Janet B. Lohman. **page 15:** *Photographer:* Jack Parsons. **page 151:** *Photographer:* Steve Gross and Susan Daley. **page 152:** *Photographer:* Nancy Hill; *Designer:* Deborah T. Lipner. **page 153:** *Photographer:* George Mattei; *Designer:* Acorn Design. **page 154:** *Photographer (top):* Jessie Walker; *Artist:* Marilyn Adamovic. *Photographer (bottom):* Jessie Walker; *Artist:* Marilyn Adamovic. **page 155:** *Photographer:* Woody Cady; *Builder/Designer:* Marcus Dubrowski, Winthrope Builders. **page 156:** *Photographer (clockwise):* Brian Vanden Brink. *Photographer:* Francis Hammond; *Designer:* piadesign. *Photographers:* Steve Gross and Susan Daley. **page 157:** *Photographers:* Steve Gross and Susan Daley. **page 158:** *Photographer:* Phillip H. Ennis. **page 160:** *Photographer:* Rob Melnychuk; *Designer:* Kelly Sanderson. **page 161:** *Photographer:* Steve Gross and Susan Daley. **page 162:** *Photographer:* Mark Lohman; *Designer:* Janet B. Lohman. **page 163:** *Photographer:* Sam Gray; *Designer:* Bierly-Drake Assoc. **page 164:** *Photographer:* Steve Gross and Susan Daley. **page 164-165:** *Photographer:* Sam Gray; *Designer:* Bierly-Drake Assoc. **page 166:** *Photographer (clockwise):* Sam Gray; *Designer:* Bierly-Drake Assoc. *Photographer:* Francis Hammond; *Designer:* piadesign. *Photographer:* Terry Wild Studio. **page 167:** *Photographer:* Rob Melnychuk; *Designer:* Wendy Williams Watt. **page 168-169:** *Photographer (clockwise):* Nancy Hill; *Designer:* David Parker. *Photographer:* Jack Parsons. *Photographer:* Steve Gross and Susan Daley. **page 170:** *Photographer:* Gay Bumgarner/Tony Stone Images. **page 171:** *Photographer:* Michael Moreland. **page 175:** *Photographer:* Lilo Raymond. **page 176:** *Photographer:* Richard Elliott/Tony Stone Images.

SOURCES

Photographers

Gordon Beall, Bethesda, MD; 301/229-0076. *Woody Cady*, Bethesda, MD; 301/656-0009. *Grey Crawford/Beate Works*; 310/558-1100. *Stephen Cridland*, Portland, OR; 503/274-0954. *Phillip Ennis*, Freeport, NY; 516/379-4243. *Mark Gibson*, Mount Shasta, CA; 916/926-5966. *Tria Giovan*, New York, NY; 212/533-6612. *Rob Gray*, New York, NY; 212/721-3240. *Sam Gray*, Boston, MA; 617/237-2711. *Gross & Daley*, New York, NY; 212/679-4606. *Anne Gummerson*, Baltimore, MD; 410/276-6936. *Kari Haavisto*, New York, NY; 212/807-6760. *Francis Hammond*, New York, NY; 212/7242800. *Nancy Hill*, Mt. Kisco, NY; 212/724-2800. *Douglas Keister*, Albany, CA; 213/558-9909. *Mark Lohman*, Los Angeles, CA; 213/933-3359; *Hal Lott*, Houston, TX; 713/439-1454. *George Mattei*, Fairfield, NJ; 973/575-9064. *Steven Mays*, New York, NY; 212/627-9121. *Bruce McCandless*, White Plains, NY; 914/948-2948. *Rob Melnychuk*, Vancouver, BC; 604/736-8066. *Melabee M Miller*, Hillside, NJ; 908/527-9121. *Mike Moreland*, Atlanta, GA; 770/993-6059. *Robert Perron*, Branford, CT; 203/481-2004. *David Phelps*, Los Angeles, CA; 213/464-7237. *Lilo Raymond*, Eddyville, NY; 914/338-8861. *Eric Roth*, Boston, MA; 617/338-5358. *Mark Samu*, Bayport, NY; 212/754-0415. *Alan Shortall*, Chicago, IL; 773/252-3747. *Holly Stickley*, Tigard, OR; 503/639-4278. *Tony Stone Images*, New York, NY; 212/545-8220. *Al Teufen*, Medina, OH; 330/723-3237. *Brian Vanden Brink*, Rockport, ME; 207/236-4035. *Terry Wild Studio*, Williamsport, PA; 717/745-3257. *Jessie Walker Associates*, Glencoe, IL; 708/835-0522. *Tom Yee*, New York, NY; 212/734-2398.

Designers, Artists, and Architects

Acorn Design, Frenchtown, NJ; 908/996-4880. *Marilyn Adamovic*, Waukegan, IL; 847/541-9643. *Arnot & McComas*, Baltimore, MD; 410234-0450. *Ron Becker*, Becker Interiors, Vienna, VA; 703/573-23-41, *Bernstein & Gold*, Victoria, BC; 250/384-7899. *Bierly-Drake Associates, Inc.*, Boston,

MA; 617/247-0081. *Eileen Boyd Design*, Huntington, NY; 516/427-6400. *Jim Brown and Matt Vanderwerff*, Vancouver, BC; 604/739-0406. *Mayo De Lucci Design*, New York, NY; 212/752-2762. *Michael DeSantis*; 516/379-4273. *Marcus Dubrowski*, Winthrope Builders, Highland, MD; 301/854-1084. *Lori Erenberg*, Pacific, Palisades, CA; 310/459-1515. *John Fortney*, San Francisco, CA; 510/526-8050. *Dennis Garritty*, Preston's Interiors, Vancouver, BC; 604/733-8345 *Gail Greene*, New York, NY; 212/909-0376. *John Hasenberg*, Portland, OR; 503/281-3313. *Karyne Johnson*, Panache Interiors, Darien, CT; 203/655-5143. *Christine Lane*, CLC Interior Design, Boston MA; 617/542-9070. *Anne McCutcheon Lewis*, McCartney Lewis Architects, Washington, DC; 202/328-0200. *Deborah T. Lipner*, Greenwich, CT; 203/629-2626. *Janet B. Lohman Interior Design*, Los Angeles, CA; 310/471-3955. *Veronique Louvet Interior Design*, Boston, MA; 617/267-5401. *Peryle Magnuson Interior Design, Ltd.*; West Vancouver, BC; 604/987-9778. *Kay McCarthy and Alfie McAdams*, Burr Ridge, IL; 630/654-0544. *Robert Miklos*, Schwartz Silver Architects, Boston, MA; 617/542-6650. *Miller/Hull Partnership*, Seattle, WA; 206/682-6837. *Rita Monaco*, Vancouver, BC; 604/876-2005. *Anne Mullin Interiors*, Greenwich, CT; 203/625-0184. *Piadesign*, New York, NY; 212/486-2021. *Kelly Sanderson*, Vancouver, BC; 604/681-3400. *Todd Schwebel*, Chicago, IL; 312/280-1998. *Sears & Sears*, A.I.A., Quogue, NY; 516/653-4218. *Richard Smith*, Sewickley, PA; 412/741-3737. *Skip Sroka*, Sroka Design, Washington, DC; 202/364-4400. *Tracey Stephens Interiors*, Montclair, NJ; 973/744-8947. *P.V. Svigals Assoc.*, New Haven, CT; 203/786-5110. *Vignette Design*, West Vancouver, BC; 604/925-1197. *Wendy Williams Watt*, Vancouver, BC; 604/684-4183. *Josette Whist*, Saltsprings Island, BC; 250/537-1048. *Gail Whiting*, 908/781-2092. *Wiseman & Gale*, Scottsdale, AZ; 602/945-8447.

Waverly, FSC Wallcoverings, New York, NY; 212/966-9000 to the trade.

INDEX

Have a home decorating, improvement, or gardening project? Look for these and other fine Creative Homeowner books wherever books are sold. . .

Projects to personalize your rooms with paint and paper. 300 color photos. 176 pp.; 9"x10"
BOOK #: 279723

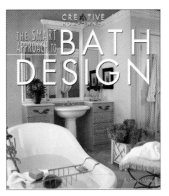

All you need to know about designing a bath. over 50 color photos. 76 pp.; 9"x0"
BOOK #: 287225

How to create kitchen style like a pro. Over 150 color photographs. 176 pp.; 9"x10"
BOOK #: 279935

How to work with space, color, pattern, texture. Over 300 photos. 256 pp.; 9"x10"
BOOK #: 279667

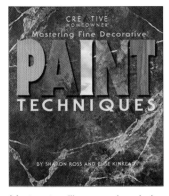

Master stenciling, sponging, glazing, marbling, and more. Over 300 illustration. 272 pp., 9"x10"
BOOK #: 279550

Original ideas for decorating and organizing kids' rooms. Over 200 illustrations. 176pp., 9"x10"
BOOK #: 279473

Design advice and industry tips for choosing window treatments. Over 225 illustrations. 176pp., 9"x10"
BOOK # 279431

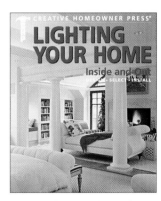

Design a lighting scheme for every room in your home and outdoors. 525 illustrations. 176 pp., $8^1/_2$"x$10^7/_8$"
BOOK #: 277583

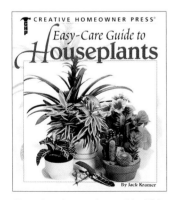

Complete houseplant guide. 200 readily available plants; more than 400 photos. 192 pp.; 9"x10"
BOOK #: 275243

Create more beautiful, healthier, lower-maintenance lawns. Over 300 illustrations. 160 pp.; 9"x10"
BOOK #: 274359

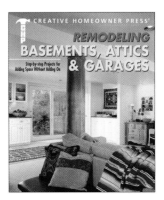

How to convert unused space into useful living area. 570 illustrations. 192 pp.; $8^1/_2$"x$10^7/_8$"
BOOK #: 277680

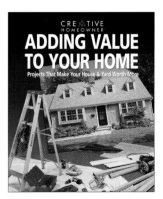

Filled with DIY projects to repair, upgrade, and add value. 500 illustrations. 176 pp.; $8^1/_2$"x$10^7/_8$"
BOOK #: 277006

For more information, and to order direct, call 800-631-7795; in New Jersey 201-934-7100.
Please visit our Web site at www.creativehomeowner.com